MEBYON KERNOW AND CORNISH NATIONALISM

Bernard Deacon, Dick Cole and Garry Tregidga

WELSH ACADEMIC PRESS

Published in Wales by Welsh Academic Press, an imprint of

Ashley Drake Publishing Ltd
PO Box 733
Cardiff
CF14 2YX

First Impression - 2003

ISBN
1 86057 0755

British Library Cataloguing-in-Publication Data.
A CIP catalogue for this book is available from the British Library.

CONTENTS

This book is dedicated to the memory of Richard Jenkin and Ron Williams and all those others who have given so much time and energy to the cause of self-government for Cornwall.

ACKNOWLEDGEMENTS

The authors would like to thank a number of people who helped to make this book a reality.

First and foremost, we would like to thank Treve Crago, who carried out interviews and transcribed much of the oral history material, Professor Philip Payton for writing the Preface, and Dr Ronald Perry and Malcolm Williams who both kindly read a draft of this book from cover to cover and made a range of helpful suggestions.

We are also grateful to the following who helped us with pieces of information on past events or commented on early drafts of the book; Loveday Carlyon, Ted Chapman, Julyan Drew, Julyan Holmes, Roger Holmes, Ann Jenkin, the late Richard Jenkin, Colin Lawry, Pedyr Prior, Donald Rawe, Ann Reynolds, Charles Thomas and George Pawley White.

The book would also be less complete without the numerous images within it, many of which were located and supplied by the following: the family of Cecil Beer (8), Birmingham Central Library (1), Chris Bowden (39, 46, 47, 49, 50, 53, 54), Mrs. L.J. Pinhay (10), George Ellis Collection at the Cornish Studies Library (9, 16, 17), Julyan Drew (38), Gorseth Kernow (2, 3, 5), Pol Hodge (44, 51), Loveday Jenkin (43), Ann Jenkin (11, 13, 14, 18, 19, 25, 31, 33), Colin Lawry (42), Sam Morgan Moore [www.photo-point.co.uk] (48) and Malcolm Williams (34, 35). Clive Wakfer meanwhile gave permission to reproduce his cartoon of Colin Lawry (41).

PREFACE

The sea change in governance in the United Kingdom of the last half decade or so, ranging from the fruits of the 'peace process' in Northern Ireland to the establishment of the Scottish Parliament and Assemblies in Wales and London, has mirrored changes in the way in which the academic community has reflected upon the history and politics of the British State. As recently as the 1970s (when I studied politics at Bristol), the United Kingdom was presented as an almost classic example of the homogenous 'civic culture' that supposedly characterised modern, mature Western states, while so-called 'British history' was essentially *English* history – or at any rate an anglocentric history which made little more than a passing nod in the general direction of what folk liked then to call 'the Celtic periphery'.

But even as political scientists were elucidating their 'civic culture', so forces and events on the ground – in Northern Ireland, in Scotland, in Wales as well as in the territorial components of other Western states such as Spain, Canada, Belgium and Italy – were pointing not to homogeneity but to diversity, the upsurge in nationalist, regionalist and anti-metropolitan sentiment challenging the conventional wisdoms that had emerged since the Second World War. In the United Kingdom, as elsewhere, political scientists had to return to the drawing board, redefining the UK as a 'multinational state' and recognising the significance of ethno-territorial issues in British politics. At the same time, historians began to look again at the history of these islands, progressively distancing themselves from the hitherto dominant anglocentric historiography and engaging instead in a new project designed to create an 'archipelagic' history which admitted the significant and distinctive roles of each of the territorial components of the 'Atlantic Archipelago' (the British Isles) in our collective experience.

In the United Kingdom, these shifts in the academic focus have launched a raft of new studies and publications, many charting the fortunes of the several nationalist, regionalist and anti-metropolitan parties and pressure groups that have in part been responsible for the re-fashioning of the twenty-first century British State. But there is one component of the UK that is routinely overlooked or misunderstood in this new rush of activity, and that is Cornwall. Although Mebyon Kernow, the Cornish national movement, has never achieved the successes achieved of Plaid Cymru and the Scottish National Party, it has influenced the conduct of politics in Cornwall to a degree that its opponents often care not to admit, while contemporary Cornwall – with its recent declaration campaign of 50,000 calling for a Cornish Assembly – is a fascinating case study of the unfinished business and unresolved tensions in the devolutionary process.

This book, therefore, not only helps to 'fill the gap' in adding to the literature on the 'parties of the periphery' (as they were called in the 1970s) but is a timely and significant contribution to our understanding of the political diversity of the modern British State. Written by a team of distinguished Cornish scholars, each of them living and working in Cornwall, it also demonstrates the extent to which Cornish Studies as a subject area has come of age, able to both learn from and contribute to the important academic debates surrounding the nature and future of the United Kingdom.

Professor Philip Payton,
Director, Institute of Cornish Studies, University of Exeter.

I

THE CORNISH PARADOX

In 1979 two American sociologists asked why there 'should be so much of a Welsh problem, yet so little of a Cornish one'.[1] The question was posed at the end of a period which had seen spectacular electoral gains for nationalist parties in Scotland and Wales. In the light of their success, the relative electoral invisibility of Mebyon Kernow (MK), the Cornish nationalist party, appeared puzzling, an anomaly waiting to be explained.

Or was it? The apparent weakness of Cornish nationalism only becomes a 'problem' for those who assume that Cornwall is a Celtic nation identical to Scotland, Wales, Ireland, Mann or Brittany and differing only in size. Exactly such an assumption was made by many, both inside and outside Cornwall, during the twentieth century. Indeed, this view of Cornwall as one of a Celtic family of nations underpinned and legitimated the emergence of MK and overt political nationalism in Cornwall after World War Two. But, however unpalatable the fact was to that small band of visionaries who set out on the long road to self-government in 1951, Cornwall has also been imagined in another, very different, way. For most people in England and, more crucially, for a large proportion even in Cornwall, Cornwall was and is felt to be an English county. It might be a distinct one, a place with special characteristics, but essentially it occupies the same conceptual space as does any county. It is just another, albeit more colourful, version of Kent or Buckinghamshire or Yorkshire. Cornwall is therefore unusual. It is a Celtic nation and yet it can also be thought of as an English county, while some people see no contradiction in it being both at the same time!

For those who see Cornwall as just another English county Hechter and Levy's question can be turned on its head. The issue becomes not why there was so little of a Cornish problem but why, as the second half of the twentieth century unfolded, there was so much of one. In 2001 MK celebrated its first half-century, during which time it had entered the electoral arena and had become a regular, if marginal, feature of Cornwall's political landscape. Its visibility east of the River Tamar may have remained indistinct, but it did all the things normally expected of political parties. It ran local campaigns, held annual meetings, contested elections, won the occasional council seat and, at the local level, garnered levels of voting support usually well in excess of those won in England by fourth parties such as the Greens or parties of the far right or far left. No other apparently English county has been the setting for a permanent political party demanding territorial devolution and some form of autonomy. Furthermore, MK is only part of a wider political movement that has, over the years, also spawned two breakaway political parties, a revived medieval institution of self-government – the Stannary Parliament, a range of less permanent pressure groups and the occasional foray into clandestine direct action. These were very unusual developments indeed, showing Cornwall to be considerably more than a mere English county. This is something that many people in England and especially in the corridors of power in London, have consistently failed to grasp.

Uncertainties about Cornwall's precise status have also influenced Cornwall's national movement itself. In consequence many members of Cornish political organisations have rejected the label 'nationalist', preferring to describe themselves as 'revivalists' or 'autonomists', a word much in vogue in the 1970s, or even sometimes 'regionalists'. While recognising these multiple self-descriptions exist, we have decided here to use the word 'nationalist' throughout. This is partly for the sake of simplicity but partly also because we feel the label is wide enough to encompass all those demanding a measure of administrative devolution or self-government for Cornwall. Nevertheless, we should also make it clear at this point that Cornish nationalism includes a wide spectrum of views on the future government of Cornwall. It is certainly a lot more sophisticated than the shorthand term 'separatist' might imply. This more pejorative label, while rejected by virtually all nationalists, is regularly invoked by political opponents, by media commentators and occasionally even by those who, in their desire for devolution of decision-making to a Cornish level, meet our definition of 'nationalist'.[2]

Nationalist movements like the Cornish, or the Welsh, Scottish or Basque come to that, also need to be distinguished from the nationalism of established states. The latter nationalism is one actively promoted by governments and ruling elites, such as British or French or American nationalism. It defends an existing political structure, is usually conservative and often centralist (especially in Europe). Such nationalisms, moreover, dominate. Their assumptions are carried daily by press and television and their view – of a world divided into 'nation-states' – is taken for granted. So much so that they often become invisible. This dominant brand of what has been described as 'banal nationalism' is very different from the nationalism of submerged peoples and nations.[3]

The latter, found in territories such as Cornwall, aims to reform over-centralised state structures, is more 'bottom-up' than 'top-down' and tends towards radicalism in its politics.

Moreover, within decentralising nationalist movements, some observers distinguish between ethnic and civic nationalism. Ethnic nationalism is first and foremost based on the defence of a distinct people and is more likely to be cultural in its orientation. Civic nationalism is more inclusive, basing its claims on the rights to citizenship of all those people living in a territory rather than on the needs of one particular ethnic group within that territory. As we shall see Cornish nationalism began with a strongly ethnic dimension but during the 1970s began to shift towards a more civic nationalism. Nevertheless, some groups active within Cornish nationalism have a more 'ethnic' approach than others and the debate between ethnic and civic nationalism was never far below the surface in MK before the 1980s.

Cornwall's ambiguous position – as a Celtic nation where nationalism has rarely succeeded in breaking through the visibility barrier and as an English county with a persistently active political nationalist movement – creates its own difficulties of explanation. In particular, Cornwall's administrative location as a county renders its national politics invisible to vast swathes of the English metropolitan chattering classes. On the other hand its 'Celticity' also attracts a romanticism that can numb rational analysis of its political history. We might conclude that neither 'Celtic nation' nor 'English county' prove very helpful categories for explaining the persistence and level of support for Cornish nationalism. So how do we begin to explain it? A good place to start is to forget about preconceived categories and ask a different question entirely. To understand the modern Cornish national movement we have to realise why Cornwall 'remains the one part of England where not all indigenous inhabitants automatically describe themselves as English'.[4] Hard evidence on the extent of this imagining is hard to come by, although the willingness of the Cornish to enter 'Cornish' in response to nationality questions suggests a cultural identity that is qualitatively much more significant than any run of the mill county or region. The 50,000 declarations collected in support of an elected assembly for Cornwall over eighteen months in 2000–2001 is also evidence that a sense of Cornishness thrives. In relative terms this is almost as high a proportion of the electorate as that which signed up to the 'Parliament for Wales' campaign in Wales in the early 1950s – and the Welsh petition was collected over a period twice as long.[5] It is the existence of this Cornish identity, remarkably surviving a thousand years of incorporation into the English state, which has both facilitated the emergence of the Cornish national movement and, at the same time, been stimulated by it.

In the remainder of this introductory chapter we survey the reasons why many people in Cornwall refuse to regard themselves as English. To do this we will have to delve back into the past. We will argue that by the end of the nineteenth century Cornwall was being imagined in a way that allowed the seeds of cultural and political nationalism to germinate and during the twentieth century to form at least a robust undergrowth if not yet flower into luxuriant foliage. Doing this establishes the setting for the history of MK and political nationalism that follows.

Cornwall's Celtic past

Part of the reason for modern Cornish nationalism lies in the facts of its history. The Cornish were one branch of those British peoples gradually, over half a millennium, subjugated by Germanic invaders. While cultural evidence of the former British inhabitants was largely erased in what was to become England this was not the case in Cornwall. On a number of dimensions, Cornwall remained a distinct entity within the medieval British Isles. Politically, it may have been ruled as part of the English kingdom, but it had gained certain 'jurisdictional particularities'.[6] Two are usually cited; Stannary courts and Parliament that grew out of the customary rights granted to tinners from 1201 onwards and the Duchy of Cornwall, established in 1337.

However, similar institutions were also found in other peripheral parts of the English state until the early 1500s. In the north and the Welsh Marches, for instance, powerful landlords wielded considerable autonomy and the writ of a London government was sometimes felt very feebly indeed. What added to Cornwall's separateness and ensured its people an intermittent status as one of the four peoples of Britain[7] was the continued existence of a spoken British language. Place-name evidence suggests that, before the tenth century and Cornwall's political incorporation into the English state, English had only displaced Cornish in the far north-east of Cornwall, while English and Cornish speaking communities lived side by side in the far south-east, adjoining the River Tamar. What had looked like an inevitable process of westwards anglicisation seems to have been decisively stopped in its tracks in the two centuries before the Norman invasion of England in 1066. Whether Athelstan's settlement of 936 reflected a less aggressive colonising policy on the part of the English, whether Cornwall proved unattractive to English settlers or whether, more likely, the attention of Wessex's ruling house was distracted northwards by the threat from Danish and Norse Vikings, the Cornish people were fortunate to have survived as a distinct entity during this critical period.

But survive they did and their future was further guaranteed by the Norman invasion. For this replaced a Saxon ruling class by a remoter landowning elite, first Breton and then Anglo-Norman, and provided the space within which the 'peculiar' institutions of Stannaries and Duchy flourished.[8] The loosely centralised political structure of medieval England and the sheer logistical difficulties of governing a land 300 miles to the west of London also furnished the opportunity for a medieval Cornish cultural renaissance. Although it shared in the fourteenth century crisis of Black Death and depopulation, Cornwall's wealth in this period grew faster, albeit from a low base, than did that of most of England. Moreover, a vigorous Cornish speaking culture flourished, based on such rituals as the miracle plays performed annually on certain saints' days at the Plain an Gwarries scattered across mid and west Cornwall. Some of these plays were written at Penryn's Glasney College, an ecclesiastical centre of literacy in the Cornish language. Indeed, some Cornish language scholars have even claimed that the Cornish language recolonised parts of east Cornwall in the late medieval period.[9] If it did so it would only have echoed what happened in other Celtic-speaking parts of the British Isles. For the Irish language recolonised parts of Ireland in the thirteenth and fourteenth centuries and Welsh did the same in parts of south Wales both then and at a later period.[10] As a result, in the early sixteenth century, after half a millennium of English rule, Cornish was still spoken in mid and west Cornwall by possibly as many as 30,000 of Cornwall's 55,000 or so inhabitants.

The persistence of this small but vigorous language community underpinned the recognition of Cornwall and the Cornish as a distinct component of the British Isles into the 1500s. The Venetian ambassador to Castile, stranded in Penryn by adverse weather in 1506, dramatically reported that: 'We are ... in the midst of a most barbarous race, so different in language and customs from the Londoners and the rest of England that they are as unintelligible to these last as to the Venetians'.[11] Similarly, in 1539 the French ambassador, perhaps succumbing to some optimistic thinking in the context of Franco-English rivalry, reported to his political masters that 'Cornwall was one of the natural enemies of England'.[12] This view may have been stimulated by the events of 1497. In that year a Cornish force rose twice against the government. The first epic rising, led by Michael Joseph 'An Gof'[13] and Thomas Flamank, reached the very outskirts of London, only to go down to defeat. It was most unusual for 'local' risings to show such strategic purpose as did the Cornish. Such a thrust into the heart of the English state dramatically brought the Cornish to the attention of the King and his counsellors and perhaps to observers even further afield, like the later French ambassador.

This ambiguous Cornish status – politically incorporated into the English realm but culturally regarded as a distinct nation – was fatally compromised by the religious Reformation of the sixteenth century and the centralising tendencies of the Tudor state. In the short run this triggered the bloody Cornish rising of 1549 when, in relative terms, as many Cornish men were killed in a few months as were French men during the four years of World War One. In the longer run it led to closer political oversight and, crucially, guaranteed the decline of the Cornish language. It was in the Cornish speaking communities of west Cornwall that Carew in the 1590s could still detect an ethnic hostility towards the English: 'fostering a fresh memory of their expulsion long ago by the English, they second the same with a bitter repining at their fellowship; and this the worst sort express in combining against and working them all the shrewd turns which … they can devise'.[14] However, by the time he was writing the Cornish language community was beginning to shrink. By the later 1600s it was in rapid decline, confined to an area west of Redruth and Falmouth and even there 'ma mouy Sousenack clappiez dre eza Curnoack, rag radden el bose keevez na el skant clappia, na guthvaz Curnooack, buz skant denveeth buz ore guthvaz ha clappia Sousenack' [*there is more English spoken than there is Cornish, for some can be found there who can hardly speak, nor understand, Cornish, but hardly anyone who cannot understand and speak English*].[15]

When the Welsh linguist Edward Lhuyd visited Cornwall around 1700 Cornish was only to be heard in a string of rural coastal parishes from St. Just in Penwith to Landewednack in the far west. By 1800 the last elderly speakers of Cornish were leaving the final ebbing traces of vernacular Cornish in the fishing port of Mousehole. Unlike Welsh, no literate lay class of Celtic language speakers had emerged before the 1550s. The gentry had deserted Cornish well before then and, in consequence, the Cornish did not follow the Welsh in translating the Bible into the local tongue in the 1560s. Cornish as a community language was doomed. It was left with a residual status, abandoned by the gentry, marginalised in trade and, finally, its close links with Brittany and the Breton language broken by the Reformation and the cutting of its European ties by a newly nationalist England. With its demise the future of the Cornish people as a distinct ethnic group looked grim. Indeed, some academics have seen the decline of the language in the sixteenth and seventeenth centuries as the final nail in the coffin of a Cornish sense of ethnicity. For Mark Stoyle the sixteenth century saw 'the end of the Cornish as a … people' while the 'spark of Cornish ethnicity [was] practically extinguished' by 1750.[16] However, they are wrong. And they are mistaken because the way people think about themselves and their identity does not just rest upon the 'facts' of history but on the ways that history is remembered.

Remembering Cornwall, recreating the Celt: Cornwall's industrial period

It became increasingly fashionable in the 1990s for writers on the Celt to debunk the idea of the 'Celtic' lands of Britain (and France). They claimed that the notion of the Celt and its associated baggage was actually conceived in the metropolitan centre and imposed upon the peasantry of the periphery in a torrid wave of romanticism.[17] It is certainly possible to identify a romantic view of Cornwall as a part of a mysterious, sullen, superstitious 'Celtic' periphery. This is a view strengthened in the late nineteenth century and the Edwardian years, when the English middle classes rediscovered Cornwall, courtesy of the Great Western Railway. In the process, they played out their suburban fantasies of the mysterious 'Other' in the far west. But, the 'post-Celtic' revisionists make a false (and patronising) assumption that things only get discovered in the 'centre' before being imposed on the periphery. This ignores the way that, much earlier in the eighteenth and early nineteenth centuries, the Cornish intelligentsia had already constructed its own ethnic history. And in searching for their own origins they had rediscovered their Celtic past well before it was 'invented' by the English.

In the 1760s William Borlase was writing of the 'Cornish Britons' who, fleeing before the Saxons, 'retired into Wales and Cornwall' and then 'into Brittany', from which bastions they maintained a perpetual struggle against the Saxons for the full space of 500 years.[18] In the early 1820s, Samuel Drew, son of a tin streamer from near St. Austell and a prominent Methodist thinker, constructed a nationalist interpretation of Cornwall's history: 'so tenacious were the British tribes of their ancient inheritance, that they disputed the encroachments of their invader, and defended their hereditary rights against them for several centuries'. Cornwall's incorporation into the Kingdom of Wessex was also constructed in recognisably nationalist terms. This was 'both fatal and final to the independence of the Cornish. This, amidst all the struggles that Cornwall made to preserve her liberty untainted, and that her enemies made to rob her of that inestimable jewel, this was the era of the first subjugation of the Cornish by the English'. The writings of Borlase and Drew, and others such as Richard Polwhele, guaranteed that notions of a vague 'golden age' of Cornish independence lingered on into the nineteenth century.[19]

At the same time, Cornwall was experiencing major economic and social change. West Cornwall was one of Europe's earliest eighteenth century industrial regions, based on the expansion of copper mining after the 1730s, adding a new dimension to the much older tradition of tin mining. Cornwall's industrial period has tended to pose a problem for insider and outsider observers alike. For some, this was the period when Cornwall became more like England. Its people adopted Methodism; they shared in the scientific and technological discourse of rationality that was sweeping across Britain; they established literary institutions, schools and political parties in ways indistinguishable from other places across Britain. This, combined with the apparent disappearance of the Cornish language, seemed to herald the submergence of a distinct Cornish identity into a greater English or British identity. Certainly, some of the 'Celtic' revivalists of the early twentieth century had more than a few difficulties with this period of Cornish history. They preferred to look back wistfully to the more romantic certainties of medieval, Cornish-speaking and Catholic Cornwall. But this fundamentally understates the crucial role of Cornwall's industrial period in the formation of the twentieth century sense of Cornishness and, more indirectly, in the emergence of political nationalism in the second half of that century. Indeed, we might go so far as to say that if there had been no eighteenth century industrialisation in Cornwall there would have been no twentieth century nationalist movement.

In the 18th century a compact industrial district grew up, centred on the parishes of Illogan, Redruth and Gwennap. Here, inventors such as Richard Trevithick and James Murdoch developed and extended the technology of the industrial revolution, particularly the steam engine. Here too, Wesleyan Methodism had found a fertile soil and had already reached membership levels never to be seen in England. In the rural industrial areas around the core district, independent communities, largely beyond the day to day influence of gentry, clergy and magistrates, were developing their own unique traditions. By the 1810s this rural-industrial society had matured. Two great Methodist revivals in 1799 and 1814 had turned Methodism into the dominant Cornish denomination. Copper mining reached new production levels on the back of high prices caused by the Napoleonic Wars and the steam engine attained levels of efficiency regarded as theoretically impossible by contemporary scientists. A culture of 'empirical tinkering', of on the job small-scale improvements and a willingness to use new techniques, had led to this state of affairs. In and around the towns an increasingly confident professional and merchant class was developing early banking facilities and investing in novel things such as the (still horse drawn) railway and new port and harbour facilities.

This industrialisation was important in two ways. First, it added new symbols of Cornish distinctiveness to the local cultural repertoire. For example, in 1847, quarrymen from Delabole, demonstrating at Wadebridge against corn exports at a time of high food prices, marched around the streets with a red flag – the symbol of spilt blood – and a pasty on a pole.[20] The pasty had become a recognisably Cornish icon. Second, it restored a sense of pride in being Cornish. The feeling of being part of a region leading the way industrially, living in a place that had developed the steam engine to a pitch of perfection, one of the people that had mastered the special skills required for deep metal mining, gave the Cornish a special pride, even conceit and arrogance, about their own capabilities. It is extremely unlikely that a national movement could ever have emerged in the twentieth century without this sentiment, one that was, in an attenuated form, to survive the long, harsh years of de-industrialisation after the early 1870s. Had Cornwall remained a largely agricultural society after the contraction of the Cornish language would sufficient momentum have existed to push-start a cultural nationalism in the early twentieth century? The answer is no. Cornish nationalism needed the foundation of its industrial experience as well as its Celtic history or its historical institutions. And this fact alone begins to explain some of the differences between Cornish and Scottish/Welsh nationalism in the late twentieth century.

Industrial pride became stitched on to other symbols of Cornishness that looked back to an earlier period and to some extent combined the world of mining and Methodism and pre-industrial Cornish-speaking Cornwall. For instance, the rapid popularisation of the song 'Trelawny', composed by Robert Stephen Hawker in the 1820s, was significant. Its popularity was a measure of the Cornish consciousness of the mid-nineteenth century, yet it harked back to semi-mythical events of the seventeenth century that kept alive a sense of Cornish resistance to the central state – 'Here's twenty thousand Cornishmen will know the reason why'! Similarly, the Cornish language itself may have ceased to be spoken, but it was not dead. It lived on in placenames, people's surnames and dialect words, too familiar to be easily forgotten. Indeed, before the language was even decently cold in its grave, antiquarians were nostalgically pining over it. Davies Gilbert, an avowed enthusiast for the new industrial age, felt in the 1820s that the best thing that had happened to the Cornish was the move from speaking Cornish to English, from a marginalised and despised tongue to the language of progress, of industrial advance. However, at the same time, Gilbert wrote nostalgic poems about Cornish place-names and edited a version of a Cornish miracle play.[21] In forgetting the Cornish language he was carefully preserving it. In the 1850s the Netherton brothers of Truro began to publish *Netherton's Cornish Almanack*. Almanacs were a common feature of industrial regions in the north of England, containing useful information interspersed with dialect stories. The interesting thing about *Netherton's Cornish Almanack* was that it included a large proportion, up to a third of the copy, in and about Cornish. This reminded a large middle class and semi-skilled working class readership of the existence of the language, even during the period which some would claim was its lowest ebb.

The Cornish language therefore retained a place in that melange of pride in industrial prowess, veneration of the steam engine, growing popularity of dialect stories and Methodist religious commitment that made up an articulated public identity by the 1840s. However, this co-existed and to some extent competed with other public identities. Most notably, there was a wider Protestant nonconformist identity. As Methodists gradually distanced themselves from the Church of England during the nineteenth century they forged stronger links with the cause of political reform and, later, the Liberal Party. The strength of Methodism in Cornwall meant that, by the 1880s, Cornwall had become one of the heartlands of Gladstonian Liberalism. This engagement with the politics of the British state also introduced other public identities. Most notably there was a sense of Britishness and a pride in Empire. Again, Cornwall's particular history of mass emigration, beginning in the 1840s and reinforced by the slump in the mining industry after the 1860s, had scattered Cornish communities across the globe, but particularly to North America and Australia. To some extent this opened the Cornish to imperialist ideas in the late nineteenth century, ideas strengthened by their involvement in emigration to South Africa's gold mining regions in the 1890s. But the large numbers of Cornish in the USA also meant that the international Cornish community stretched beyond the British Empire. These communities, dispersed across far-flung mining frontiers, maintained a sense of pride in Cornish industrial prowess. Moreover, through return migration, they acted as reservoirs that 'topped-up' Cornish identity. Thus, the self-image of the Cornish in Cornwall was replenished at the very same time as economic depression began to undermine the reality of industrial achievement.

Cornishness – a hybrid identity

By the 1880s, therefore, a hybrid identity had been created, with a number of potentially conflicting elements. On the one hand there was a constant, banal 'flagging' of Cornishness. At almost every public meeting on every conceivable subject the audience was being addressed as 'Cornishmen' [sic]. Aspiring parliamentary candidates fell over each other in their eagerness to prove their Cornish credentials, even if they had none. And newspaper columns were full of the everyday reminders of regional identity. However, at the same time, the dominant imagining of Cornwall had become that of an English county. This was reinforced as the century drew to a close through the new administrative arrangement of

County Councils, established in 1889. The coincidence that Cornwall's size was just about that of an average English county now took on greater significance. For the committed nationalist Cornwall's geography had played a cruel card as it appeared to legitimate its county status. This combination of a strong sense of Cornish identity, but a dominant representation of 'county' status, resulted in a strong cultural identity co-existing with a weak political one, a problem that remained to haunt the twentieth century nationalist movement. The strength of cultural identity was singularly illustrated in 1908 when Cornwall won the English county [*sic*] rugby union championships but did so with a scale and depth of public support unique in 'England'. Thousands of Cornish people turned out to watch and support their team as the latter acted like a lightning conductor for the intense cultural identity established during the nineteenth century. Such a level of support was much more akin to the support given to national sides than that of a mere county – a point sports writers in the metropolitan media continually puzzled over as similar episodes occurred intermittently through the twentieth century.

Yet this vibrant identity was slow to translate into the political arena. As an example, in 1881 a movement sprang up demanding the Sunday closing of public houses in Cornwall. The aim of this nonconformist-led campaign was to emulate Scotland, Ireland and Wales and obtain the right to a local option for a 'dry' Sunday. The campaign won ready support and within four months collected a mammoth petition of 121,000 names. Its supporters made much of the analogy with Wales and argued for parity of treatment. References were made at public meetings to Cornwall's 'Celtic blood' and the similarities between Principality and Duchy. Nevertheless, even the campaign's keenest supporters could not escape the assumption that Cornwall was a 'county'. Consequently, they never convincingly answered the claims of opponents that this was 'piecemeal', 'partial' or even 'parochial' legislation. The logic of their claims for parity with the 'sister kingdoms' of Scotland, Ireland and Wales was, when the crunch came, not followed through. Ultimately, despite their differences, 'Cornish people were very happy to be united to England, and they did not wish for Home Rule'.[22]

In this hybrid identity, therefore, imaginings of (Celtic) difference combined with that of being an English county. Cultural distinctiveness accompanied political integration and meant it was difficult to fashion a distinct political voice for Cornwall. Public identities of Englishness, Britishness, Imperialism and Protestantism overwhelmed that of Cornishness. Nonetheless, there remained throughout the nineteenth century an almost subterranean sense of Cornwall being 'not of England'. Local writers and newspaper editors were aware of this discourse but usually equally dismissive of it, sometimes viewing it as an attempt by outsiders to diminish Cornwall's status, just another version of the metropolitan myth of Cornwall as 'West Barbary'. Yet the notion of Cornwall as non-English stubbornly persisted despite respectable fears.[23] Indeed, it was fuelled by antiquarian interests in the Cornish language and by those new romantic representations of Cornwall as a 'primitive' periphery that English novelists and writers were increasingly prone to adopt as the new century dawned.

Furthermore, de-industrialisation, depopulation and the onset of chronic economic problems had, by the early twentieth century, established the preconditions for a re-imagining of Cornwall and Cornishness. As the structural economic problems of a contracting mining industry refused to solve themselves, representations of Cornwall as a centre of industrial prowess were becoming ever more threadbare. Hesitatingly, people began to look to alternative political frameworks to solve Cornwall's chronic economic problems. For a small number it slowly became clear that Cornwall's status as a county could no longer guarantee economic security and a future for its people. In contrast, this status seemingly condemned Cornwall to a future as an impoverished periphery. As older self-representations crumbled and dissolved, other sources of identity took on more prominence. It was in these conditions that Cornish men and women began to look anew at persistent notions of Cornwall as 'not of England' as they began the slow process of reasserting themselves as Cornish Celts.

Notes

1. Michael Hechter and Margaret Levi (1979), 'The Comparative Analysis of Ethno-Regional Movements', *Ethnic and Racial Studies*, Vol. 2/3, pp. 262–274.
2. For example, Andrew George, probably the closest Cornwall has come to having a 'nationalist' Member of Parliament, in an attempt to distance himself from the word 'nationalist' has written of the 'tiny handful of certifiable nationalists who want Cornwall to be "cut-off" from the rest of the world' (*Western Morning News*, 7 December 1999). Such mythical nationalists are actually very difficult to identify in practice.
3. Michael Billig (1995), *Banal Nationalism*, London. Some in the Cornish movement prefer to call this state nationalism 'statism'.
4. Bryan Ward-Perkins (2000), 'Why did the Anglo-Saxons not become more British?', *English Historical Review*, Vol. CVX. 462, pp. 513–533.
5. Linda McAllister (2001), *Plaid Cymru; The Emergence of a Political Party*, Bridgend, p. 99.
6. Michael Braddick (2000), *State Formation in Early Modern England c1550–1700*, Cambridge, p. 353.
7. Polydore Vergil, cited in Philip Payton (1992), *The Making of Modern Cornwall*, Redruth, p. 57.
8. Philip Payton (1996), *Cornwall*, Fowey, p. 100.

 9. N.J.A. Williams (1995), *Cornish Today: An Examination of the Revived Language*, Sutton Coldfield, p. 81.
10. Geraint Jenkins (ed.) (1997), *The Welsh Language Before the Industrial Revolution*, Cardiff, pp. 97 and 420.
11. Cited in A.L. Rowse (1941), *Tudor Cornwall*, London, p. 117.
12. Mary Robertson (1989), '"The Art of the Possible": Thomas Cromwell's Management of West Country Government', *The Historical Journal*, Vol. 32.4, pp. 793–816.
13. The name 'An Gof,' now spelt Angove, means 'The Smith' in English.
14. Richard Carew (1811: originally published 1602), *Survey of Cornwall*, London, p. 184.
15. Nicholas Boson, cited in Oliver Padel (1975), *The Cornish Writings of the Boson Family*, Redruth, p. 25.
16. Mark Stoyle (1999), 'The Dissidence of Despair: Rebellion and Identity in Early Modern Cornwall', *Journal of British Studies*, Vol. 38, pp. 423–444.
17. Malcolm Chapman (1992), *The Celts: The Construction of a Myth*, London.
18. William Borlase (1769: originally published 1754), *Antiquities, History and Monuments of the County of Cornwall*, London, pp. 40–44.
19. Fortescue Hitchens and Samuel Drew (1824), *The History of Cornwall*, Helston, pp. 12 and 725. See also Richard Polwhele (1806), *The History of Cornwall*, London.
20. *West Briton*, 21 May 1847.
21. Davies Gilbert(ed), *Mount Calvary, translated by John Keigwin*, London, 1826, pp. v–ix.
22. *West Briton*, 10 November 1881.
23. See, for example, the report of a lecture on Cornish Names and Nationality at St.Day in 1867 (*West Briton*, 1 February) and the debate in the letters columns of later issues.

II

THE HISTORICAL LEGACY: NATIONALISM BEFORE MK

The early years of Mebyon Kernow can only be understood within the context of the wider history of the Celto-Cornish Revival. By the early 1900s antiquarian interest in the language, folklore and archaeology of Cornwall had generated sufficient momentum for the creation of the Cowethas Kelto-Kernuak (Celtic-Cornish Society). Although this organisation had apparently folded by the outbreak of the First World War, the Revivalists went on to establish the Federation of Old Cornwall Societies by 1925 and held the first Gorseth Kernow in 1928. The existence of such cultural institutions might be regarded as the essential prerequisite for a fully-fledged nationalist movement. Yet in the Cornish case a pronounced concentration on culturalism, particularly in regard to the language issue, had the effect of delaying what might otherwise have been a natural progression to political issues. The antiquarian mould of the Revival actually produced separate strands of activity in the early twentieth century, with the efforts of leading pioneers like Henry Jenner and Robert Morton Nance focused on the practical task of reviving the Cornish language while the political dimension was occasionally adopted by some individuals on the margins of Revivalism. Despite sporadic attempts to redefine Cornish nationalism before the Second World War, the formative years of Mebyon Kernow were to prove that a coherent synthesis of politics and culture had still not taken place.

Cornwall and the Celtic Revival

The revival of the Cornish language was central to the activities of Cowethas Kelto-Kernuak (CKK) in the opening decade of the twentieth century. At the Pan-Celtic Congress in August 1901 the majority of delegates had voted to postpone a decision on recognising Cornwall as a Celtic nation since they had serious doubts as to whether Cornish could still be regarded as a living language. The symbolic importance of this issue gave added impetus to the aim of the CKK to publish a Cornish grammar and an English-Cornish dictionary. Led initially by Louis C. Duncombe-Jewell, who served as the first honorary secretary, the group now campaigned to win Celtic status for Cornwall. Reports in Cornish newspapers, combined with an angry exchange of letters in *Celtia* between Duncombe-Jewell and Lord Castletown, the president of the Celtic Association, ensured that the Celto-Cornish Revival became a serious subject for discussion.[1] In 1904 Henry Jenner, who had emerged as the leading spokesman of the society, addressed the Congress with a speech entitled 'Cornwall: A Celtic Nation' and Cornwall was formally accepted as a member of the Celtic Association. Apart from stressing the importance of reviving the Cornish language, the agenda of CKK covered a number of related cultural objectives:

1. To preserve from damage and destruction and to study the stone-circles, cromlechs, menhirs, hut circles, beehive dwellings, camps, hill forts, castles, logan and crick stones, crosses, oratories, holy wells, cemeteries, barrows, and inscribed stones.
2. To keep carefully every National Custom and above all the truly Cornish sports of Wrestling and Hurling, by presenting every year a Belt to be contended for by Cornish wrestlers, and inscribed silver Hurling balls to each Parish in the Duchy that will ordain an annual Hurling match on its feast day.
3. To revive the Cornish Language as a spoken tongue, by publishing a grammar and Dictionary of the Language, by printing all Cornish manuscripts not yet printed, by giving prizes for fresh competitions in Cornish, by paying a premium for teaching Cornish to Schoolmasters able to satisfy the Council of their fitness, and also
4. by reviving the ancient Cornish Miracle Plays and re-establishing the Cornish Gorsedd of the Bards at Boscawen-Un.[2]

Significantly, there was no direct reference to any political ambitions for the society. A combination of factors ensured that the Revivalists pursued a narrow definition of Cornish nationalism. In the first place it has been claimed that religious issues made it difficult for the Celtic movement to reach out to the wider community. Philip Payton has contrasted the success of the Welsh Revivalists, 'who managed to address their aspirations' to the nonconformist majority, with the failure of the Cornish movement to appeal to the 'mass of Cornish people'. Some of the leading figures associated with early Cornish Revivalism were either Roman Catholics, such as Jenner and Duncombe Jewell, or else High Anglicans like the Rev. W.S. Lach-Szyrma and the Rev. G.H. Doble. The romantic

objective of these individuals was to 'rebuild a pre-industrial Celtic-Catho-
lic culture in Cornwall', thereby alienating the movement from the practical and spiritual interests of the population as a whole.[3] Yet Cornish
Revivalism was sometimes combined with Free Church beliefs. Even in
the 1890s the Rev. Mark Guy Pearce, the well-known author and Wesleyan
preacher, took a great pride in being able to say the Lord's Prayer in
Cornish.[4] As we shall see, during the years leading up to the First World
War there are examples of Cornish Methodists co-opting the Celtic imagery of the Revival into their own political and religious agenda.

Scholars looking at this period have also commented on the negative
attitude of the Cornish public, with Amy Hale focusing on the concern of
the local press over a possible language revival and Ronald Perry pointing
to the need for activists to 'issue disclaimers that there was no hidden
agenda and that the study of Cornish ... was just a harmless exercise'.[5]
This desire for a respectable image reflected the fact that the Council of the
CKK was dominated by distinguished landowners and antiquarians like
Sir W.L. Salisbury-Trelawny, Thomas Robins Bolitho and John Davies
Enys. Since the 'county establishment' tended to have Conservative or
Liberal Unionist sympathies this was hardly an ideal environment for the
discussion of Cornwall's place in any future programme of constitutional
reform. Indeed, it appears that the Unionist arguments against a federal
United Kingdom were accepted by many of the leading Revivalists.
Thurstan Collins Peter, a founder member of the organisation, declared in
1906 that 'we have no desire to see Cornwall aping the larger countries of
Ireland, Wales and Brittany in their efforts after what they mistakenly sup-
pose will lead to home rule'.[6] Henry Jenner took a similar line and claimed that
there was 'no wish on anyone's part to translate the Irish political expression
'Sinn Fein' into Cornish, to agitate for Home Rule for Cornwall ... foment
disloyalty to England's King or to the British Empire'.[7]

Developments after the First World War confirmed the antiquarian
nature of the core Revival. The creation of the Federation of Old Cornwall
Societies in 1925 represented a serious attempt to disseminate the ideas
of the movement to a wider audience, with the emphasis being placed on
linking the popular interest in dialect sketches and local history to the
preservation of the Celtic identity of Cornwall. By 1935 Robert Morton
Nance, President of the Federation, was expressing his concern that
some local societies were even neglecting their cultural role. He added
that the movement was attracting 'people who will never learn, or do, or
collect, anything, but at the same time join a society because it is a
Cornish one and they have a vague Cornish sentiment'.[8] The annual
Gorseth Kernow, which first met at Boscawen-Un in 1928, was also intended as a 'medium between academic scholarship and popular culture'. Its very creation was symbolic of the appeal of romantic

nationalism, with its bardic ceremonies and references to the legendary return of King Arthur. Jack Clemo's comments on the 1933 Gorseth sum up the escapist nature of the event: 'I know of no ceremony or function which makes one forget so completely the present world muddle – which enables one to glimpse so clearly the past from which we have come'.[9] While the Revivalist mainstream immersed itself in a particular version of Cornish culture, nationalist politics was left to a minority on the fringes of the movement.

It is instructive to compare political nationalism in Cornwall with the situation in the other Celtic nations. For example, the Breton movement had become politicised by the end of the nineteenth century leading to the emergence of autonomist groups, such as the PNB (Parti Nationaliste Breton).[10] In the United Kingdom the debate over Home Rule for Ireland in the 1880s can be regarded as the catalyst for the rise of nationalism in both Scotland and Wales. The Liberal Party, weakened by the defection of the Liberal Unionists, was anxious to make constitutional reform more relevant to mainland Britain and encouraged the people of Scotland and Wales to demand a federal system of government: 'Home Rule All Round'. A Scottish Home Rule Association was formed in 1886 and support for devolution 'steadily mounted' in local Liberal Associations and the early Labour movement.[11] Similar developments took place in Wales. After 1886 a nationalist movement, Cymru Fydd, flourished within the Liberal Party under the leadership of Welsh MPs like Tom Ellis and David Lloyd George. Although the collapse of Cymru Fydd led to a period of stagnation for the nationalist cause, the years leading up to the First World War saw a renewed interest in Home Rule and the disestablishment of the Anglican Church in Wales.[12]

The legacy of the pre-war years was that a nationalist tradition had been created in both Wales and Scotland. In the 1920s disillusionment with the London-based parties led to the emergence of Plaid Cymru (1925) and the National Party of Scotland (1928). In retrospect this was a critical development. Electoral change after the First World War, described by the historian Chris Cook as the primary 'Age of Alignment' in British politics, led to a new class-based electoral system with the Labour Party replacing the Liberals as the main alternative to the Conservatives.[13] Although the Liberals survived as a major force in much of rural Wales and Scotland, this period of realignment created an opportunity for organised nationalism, preparing ground for the rise of Plaid Cymru and SNP after the Second World War. Wales, in particular, was a good example of this process. Laura McAllister points out that before 1945 Plaid Cymru 'could hardly be termed a party according to conventional definitions'.[14] During the first twenty years of its history it struggled to develop a secure niche in Welsh politics and entered the post-war period without a single elected representative. Nonetheless, its mere existence as a campaigning force for Welsh nationalism, combined with a membership of 6,000, a local branch structure and a small core staff of paid employees, meant that Plaid Cymru at least had a basis on which to build.

The emergence of anti-metropolitanism

The nationalist impulse of the pre-First World War period was much more muted in Cornwall. In consequence the conditions had not been established for building an initial base for political nationalism in the inter-war period, as happened in Scotland and Wales. This was partly due to the culturalism of the Revivalist leadership and partly to more general uncertainties about Cornish identity and nationhood. Nevertheless, it would be a mistake to assume that Cornwall was totally immune to developments taking place elsewhere in the Celtic world. Echoes of the same process could be heard but the cultural and political context in Cornwall meant that it had a different outcome. It is perhaps surprising that the imagery of the Celto-Cornish Revival, apparently a marginal force in Cornwall during the Edwardian period, actually began to filter through to a wider audience. The Liberal Party, in particular, recognised the benefits of co-opting the theme of Celtic identity for electoral purposes. In January 1910 David Lloyd George on an election visit to Falmouth declared that the Cornish and the Welsh shared the 'same Celtic passion for liberty' and described the meeting, to the cheers of the crowd, as a 'gathering of his fellow [Celtic] countrymen'.[15] During the same month the Hon. Thomas C. Agar Robartes, Liberal MP for St. Austell, took a similar view when he concluded that the 'chief characteristic of Cornishmen is their love of independence. As a nation we dislike being trampled on'.[16]

Robartes' symbolic use of the word 'nation' suggests that a public reappraisal of Cornwall's identity was taking place at this time. This appears to be confirmed by subjective evidence from oral history interviews with George Pawley White, a founder member of MK, who was born in Penzance in 1907. During his personal testimony he consistently emphasises that his family were aware of the importance of their Cornish identity before the First World War and that this sense of difference set them somehow apart from being English. His earliest childhood memories are filled with his father's emphasis that the family's Cornishness and Celticity were something different from what existed on the other side of the River Tamar, as he illustrated when reminiscing about family trips to visit his maternal grandparents who had moved to South Wales for economic reasons:

> We used to be taken to South Wales once or twice every year
> and I can always remember my father saying to me when we
> were going over the railway bridge at Saltash, 'be careful here,
> he said, you are going into England now and you must behave
> yourself!' And when we got half way through the Severn Tunnel
> going into Wales he said 'its all right, you can relax now. We are
> in Wales'. So I always knew that I wasn't English.[17]

Pawley White's acquisition of a Cornish cultural identity in his early
childhood years was closely linked to the world of party politics. Both of
his parents were 'very active Liberals' and from an early age he remembers assisting them in sending out election communications to voters.
Growing up in this radical political environment it was not surprising that
Pawley White should initially embrace the Liberal cause. Later, during
the inter-war period he combined an active role in both Cornish Liberalism and Methodism with a growing interest in the Celtic Revival by going
along to some of the early Gorseths and noting with satisfaction the
formation of Tyr ha Tavas, the Cornish group of the 1930s. This personal
fusion of Celtic Revivalism and centre-left politics meant that Pawley
White could easily eventually move over to MK:

> I knew Isaac Foot [MP for Bodmin, 1922–24 and 1929–35]
> very well and Sir Donald Maclean [MP for North Cornwall,
> 1929–32]. I went around stomping the ground for him up in
> North Cornwall. And then I was quite active in the Liberal Party
> … long before the war! And when we decided to form Mebyon
> Kernow I thought this is what I've been waiting for. This is what
> I had looked for all my life. I am not going to get this out of the
> Liberal Party or any of the English Parties, so my political memo-
> ries go right back a long way.[18]

Pawley White shows that, by the 1930s, religious nonconformity and
radical politics were no longer incompatible with Cornish nationalism.
Yet in Cornwall the home of Methodism and radicalism was Liberalism. It
is interesting to note that within the above passage of narrative Pawley
White still appears to make a clear distinction between the Liberals and
the other 'English' mainstream political parties. His formative knowledge
of party politics came from the pre- and inter-war periods when the Liberals, with their appeal to nonconformist and radical interests, were able to
present themselves as the traditional defenders of Cornish society. Even
before the First World War the local Liberals were reinforcing this regionalist role by absorbing political ideas from the other Celtic Revivals. In
1910 Sir Arthur Quiller-Couch, a leading Cornish Liberal and interestingly

a founder member of CKK, defended the cause of Irish Home Rule on pan-Celtic grounds, while Liberal activists were starting to echo their counterparts in Wales by calling for the Cornish disestablishment of the Anglican Church on the grounds that there were 'few arguments – if any – which were applied to Welsh disestablishment … which could not be applied with equal reason to Cornwall'.[19] When Winston Churchill proposed the creation of regional legislatures for England in 1912, Alfred Browning Lyne, a prominent Liberal activist and the editor of the *Cornish Guardian* newspaper, called for domestic self-government:

> There is another Home Rule movement on the horizon. Self-government for Cornwall will be the next move … We [have] considerable sympathy with the protest of these fiery Celts against the excessive centralisation, not only of Government but of culture in these days. The Metropolis is coming to mean everything, and all the provinces approximate towards the fashion of the centre … We think this is much to be deplored, and we do not see why Cornwall should not join in the 'Regionalist' movement which is striving in various parts of Western Europe to revive local patriotism.[20]

Lyne's comments point to a fusion of cultural and political nationalism. Subsequent editorials in the *Cornish Guardian*, including an appeal for a 'delegation of power' in order to address local economic issues and references to the 'Celtic temperament' of Cornish Methodism, point to a growing interest in the subject.[21] Although on the margins of the Revivalist movement, his Liberal beliefs, in contrast to the Unionist instincts of the CKK, enabled him to develop a coherent nationalist position that was relevant to the needs of pre-war Cornwall. However, the outbreak of the First World War removed those conditions that had allowed these anti-metropolitan ideas to flourish. British politics became increasingly London-centred after 1914 and it was not until the 1960s that devolution again became a major topic at Westminster. The loss of this external stimulus was crucial. Cornwall, in contrast to the other Celtic nations, lacked a recent tradition of nationalist politics and Lyne's agenda had not developed sufficiently during the pre-war period to make a lasting impact on the region's political culture.

Nonetheless, the potential for some form of nationalist politics continued after the war. The Cornish experience during the inter-war period needs to be considered against the background of Labour's historic breakthrough in British politics. Although Cornwall was initially at the forefront in the rise of socialism, with Labour polling a respectable vote in the West Cornwall constituencies in 1918, this challenge was not sustained, partly due to the deteriorating economic situation in the local tin mining industry. By 1923 radical politics was again focused on the traditional agenda of the Liberal/nonconformist alliance and the socialists remained in third place until 1950.[22] The Liberals, still entrenched as the main alternative to Conservatism, attempted to consolidate their support by pursuing an anti-metropolitan line. Only Liberalism it was argued, in contrast to the new Labour-Conservative alignment at Westminster, could 'understand Cornish folk and be in sympathy with their traditions and outlook on life'.[23] Lyne, now the chairman of Bodmin Liberal Association, developed this anti-metropolitan theme when he wrote in 1923 that Isaac Foot was the natural champion of Cornwall. He added that the region was 'a long way from London and unless the powers that be are made to realise that Cornwall does really exist ... we shall not get what is our proportion of public expenditure'.[24]

This regionalist outlook was particularly evident at the time of the 1929 election which ensured that the electoral isolation of Cornwall was more starkly portrayed than before. While the Liberals were triumphant in all five Cornish constituencies, they remained firmly in third place at Westminster. The idea that 'Good Old Cornwall' was now the 'last refuge of Liberalism' created an inward-looking attitude on the part of many Liberal activists. This was complemented by the decision of the region's MPs to form a Duchy Committee, sometimes known as the Duchy Parliamentary Group, in order to 'promote the interests of Cornwall'. By working together the five MPs could strengthen their position by claiming that they formed a united group that was defending Cornish interests at Westminster.[25] Yet interestingly the 1929 election also witnessed a challenge to all three London-based parties. John Carah Roberts, a county councillor, contested Camborne as a 'Cousin Jack Independent' on the grounds that the area was being neglected by central government. Although polling just 6.3 per cent of the vote, his campaign, symbolised by the slogan 'A Cornishman for a Cornish Constituency', pointed to the continuing development of an anti-metropolitan agenda.[26]

Such events seemed irrelevant to the antiquarian interests of the cultural Revivalists. Leading figures like Jenner were indifferent to the increasingly divergent nature of Cornish politics from the Westminster model and it appears they did not even consider the possibility of advancing their ideas through the political process. Besides, their perception of Celto-Cornish nationality had to remain separate from the wider world of party politics since its ideological inheritance was derived from the antiquarianism of the previous century. Even the full cultural potential of the language revival itself was not recognised by some individuals. A good example was Robert Morton Nance, Jenner's successor as Grand Bard, who thought that a popularisation of the movement, on the

model of Plaid Cymru, was simply not possible. In the 1930s Nance declared that 'Cornish is never likely to become a language that comes by
nature, as it were, to Cornish people. It is never likely to become useful to
a political party who could make a nuisance of it, either ...'[27]

Cornish Nationalism in the 1930s

Yet for younger Revivalists there was an increasing recognition of the
need to engage with mainstream party politics. Associated with this
development was the formation of Tyr ha Tavas (Land and Language) in
1932, which reflected a growing disenchantment amongst a new generation of activists over the antiquarian direction of the Revival. Led by
Edmund Hambly, a medical student at St. Bartholomew's Hospital but
originally from North Cornwall, Tyr ha Tavas provided a forum for young
Cornish exiles in London to exchange ideas using the Cornish language
as far as possible. The group's main priority was to make Cornwall's
language and culture more accessible to the general public and a variety
of activities were organised, including summer camps and annual church
services in Cornish. Its constitution stated that Tyr ha Tavas was 'an
organisation to unite those persons of Cornish birth or descent who
value their Cornish heritage and who desire to maintain the outlook,
individualism, culture and idealism that characterises their race so as to
pass on the unbroken tradition. The primary aim is service to Cornwall
and Cornish people and in particular it seeks:

> a. To preserve in the youth of Cornwall a love and under-
> standing of their country and its history.
> b. To encourage an expression in drama, music art, literature
> and cultural forms, of the innate Cornish instinct.
> c. To encourage the practice of typical Cornish sports.
> d. To utilise the Cornish language both as an outward and
> visible sign of nationality, and as a means of helping Cornish
> people to realise their essential kinship with other Celtic na-
> tions. To show Cornish people what Cornishmen have done and
> what they can still do to help the world.'[28]

Tyr ha Tavas represented an important stage in the evolution of Cornish
nationalism. Although ostensibly a language pressure group, it placed a
greater emphasis on practical issues. Members of the group were encouraged to take an active interest in the socio-economic 'conditions
and industry of the motherland and it was their desire to see that the
education, the daily and industrial life ... was the best that Cornwall

could provide.'[29] But some younger members of Tyr ha Tavas, notably Francis Cargeeg and Ernest Retallack Hooper, more commonly known by his bardic name of Talek (see Appendix), wanted the organisation to adopt a more distinct political agenda, thereby copying Plaid Cymru which linked the defence of the Welsh language to the political goal of self-government. Interestingly, both men were associated with the Labour movement. Cargeeg was an active trade unionist at Plymouth dockyard during these years and was concerned with the social problems of his native Cornwall. In 1932, the same year that Tyr ha Tavas was founded, Talek proposed in *Cornish Labour News* that the Labour Party should embrace a new 'Cornish Social-ism' based on a fusion of social justice and cultural nationalism. The next Labour government should pursue a locally-based approach to the socio-economic problems of Cornwall and actively support the nation's Celtic heritage. Appropriately enough, he concluded with the slogan 'Omseveagh why gonesugy Kernow!' (Arise workers of Cornwall!).[30]

Talek's call came at a time when the Labour Party was itself attempting to portray a distinctly Cornish image. It was a development that was closely associated with the political career of A.L. Rowse, Fellow of All Souls and Labour parliamentary candidate for Penryn-Falmouth through-out the 1930s. Rowse, emerging as the effective leader of the Cornish Labour movement, felt that it was essential for his party to adapt its message to local conditions. In order to make a sustained breakthrough Labour needed to stress its continuity with the old Radical cause and express a wider commitment to the Cornish way of life, both economically and socially. *Cornish Labour News*, a monthly magazine, was estab-lished to promote these ideas, with Claude Berry, a journalist and author, as its first editor. Articles on local economic problems, such as unem-ployment and the plight of the Cornish fishing industry, went alongside items of historical or cultural interest.[31] Rowse also took an interest in the development of Tyr ha Tavas. In 1937 he declared that 'all that I want to be is a spokesman for the Cornish people'. He added that if Tyr ha Tavas was serious in its talk about 'Cornwall for the Cornish [and] the particular character of the Cornish people', they should give him their support because he represented their only chance of there being a Cornish Prime Minister.[32] One interesting individual to support Rowse was John Legonna, an early advocate of Cornish self-government. In 1938 Legonna served as a platform speaker at Labour meetings in the St. Austell area and was apparently proposed by the divisional secre-tary as a candidate for Penryn-Falmouth in the event of Rowse's retire-ment from active politics.[33]

Yet the fragile foundations of this Labour-Nationalist nexus were soon undermined. To start with there was no obvious champion of Cornish Socialism once Rowse finally stood down as a candidate in the early

1940s. Claude Berry had already resigned as editor of *Cornish Labour News* and on the Revivalist side nobody came forward to take an active part in Cornish politics, though Edmund Hambly subsequently became a Labour councillor on London County Council.[34] Legonna was now turning away from mainstream politics. Towards the end of 1938 he resigned from the Labour Party over Britain's failure to intervene in the Spanish Civil War and he embraced Hugh MacDiarmid's vision of a Celtic federation of socialist republics. In 1940 Legonna refused to serve in the armed forces unless the Cornish and Welsh nations were granted self-government and he subsequently travelled through Cornwall on a bicycle in a desperate search for a refuge. Only Cargeeg really supported his 'Cornwall First' viewpoint, with other Revivalists, including Morton Nance, adopting an 'Establishment' attitude, as he put it, towards the war.[35] Although developments during the Second World War were to reveal the existence of other political nationalists, it was evident that the brief era of Talek's Cornish Socialism had drawn to a close.

The negative response to Legonna also highlights the fundamental problems confronting Cornish nationalism at this time. Even Tyr ha Tavas, with its commitment to the task of popularising the Revival, was unable to fully embrace a political agenda. Cecil Beer (see Appendix), in particular, wanted the group to avoid a 'wildcat' image. He believed that an active involvement in politics in the 1930s would have prevented members from concentrating on cultural priorities. Echoing the earlier approach of CKK he persuaded J.W. Hunkin, the Bishop of Truro, and Sir John Langdon Bonython, a wealthy Cornish exile in South Australia, to become patrons of the group.[36] This desire for respectability was yet another reason for remaining non-political. In any case, Tyr ha Tavas was simply in no position to become a pressure group for the embryonic cause of Cornish Socialism. Roughly two-thirds of its membership was scattered outside Cornwall and the group effectively became moribund at the outbreak of the Second World War.[37] Once again the absence of an institutional framework was critical. A common theme, from Lyne to Legonna, was the need for a permanent and locally based organisation that could articulate and develop nationalist ideas in a Cornish context.

Notes

1. For a discussion of the early years of Cowethas Kelto-Kernuak see Amy Hale (1997), 'Genesis of the Celto-Cornish Revival? L.C. Duncombe-Jewell and the Cowethas Kelto-Kernuak', *Cornish Studies: Five*, Exeter, pp. 100–12.
2. *Celtia* (May 1902).
3. Philip Payton (1992), *The Making of Modern Cornwall: Historical Experience and the Persistence of 'Difference'*, Redruth, p. 132.

4. Arthur Lawrence (1899), 'Rev. Mark Guy Pearce', *Cornish Magazine*, Vol. 2, pp. 243–52.
5. Hale (1997), 'Genesis', p. 105; Ronald Perry (1997), 'Celtic Revival and Economic Development in Edwardian Cornwall', *Cornish Studies: Five*, Exeter, p. 117.
6. Thurstan Peter (1906), *A Compendium of the History and Geography of Cornwall*, London, p. 202.
7. Henry Jenner (1926), 'Who are the Celts and what has Cornwall to do with them?', *Old Cornwall*, 1.
8. Robert Morton Nance to Cecil Beer, 24 June 1935, Gorseth Kernow Archive, Cornwall Record Office.
9. *Cornish Guardian*, 31 August 1933.
10. Jean Bothorel (2001), *Un Terroriste Breton*, Paris, p. 43.
11. H.J. Hanham (1969), *Scottish Nationalism*, London, pp. 99–107.
12. K.O. Morgan (1970), *Wales in British Politics, 1868–1922*, Cardiff; J. Graham Jones (1987), 'E.T. John and Welsh Home Rule, 1910–14', *The Welsh History Review/ Cylchgrawn Hanes Cymru*, Vol. 13, 4, pp. 453–67.
13. Chris Cook (1975), *The Age of Alignment: Electoral Politics in Britain, 1922–1929*, London.
14. Laura McAllister (2001), *Plaid Cymru: The Emergence of a Political Party*, Bridgend, p. 25.
15. *West Briton*, 7 and 13 January 1910.
16. *West Briton*, 7 and 21 January 1910.
17. Interview with George Pawley White, 25 January 2000, Cornish Audio Visual Archive (CAVA), Institute of Cornish Studies.
18. Pawley White, 14 September 2001, CAVA.
19. *Cornish Guardian*, 16 December 1910; *Royal Cornwall Gazette*, 24 February 1910 and 29 February 1912.
20. *Cornish Guardian*, 6 September 1912.
21. *Cornish Guardian*, 20 September 1912, 13 and 20 February 1914.
22. Garry Tregidga (1999), 'Socialism and the Old Left: The Labour Party in Cornwall during the Inter-War Period', *Cornish Studies: Seven*, Exeter, pp. 74–93.
23. Electoral address of the Liberal candidate for Penryn-Falmouth in 1935, Penryn-Falmouth Conservative Association Papers, DDX/551/11, Cornwall Record Office.
24. *Cornish Guardian*, 16 February 1923.
25. *Cornish Guardian*, 6 June 1929 and 16 January 1930; *Western Morning News*, 6 March 1930.
26. *West Briton*, 27 May and 6 June 1929.
27. Robert Morton Nance (c. 1936), 'The Cornish Language', *The Cornish Guide*, Truro, p. 18.
28. Undated Tyr ha Tavas papers at the Institute of Cornish Studies (University of Exeter).
29. *Cornish Guardian*, 30 May 1935.
30. *Cornish Labour News*, 3 (December 1932).
31. *Cornish Labour News*, issues 1–6 (1932–33).
32. *Cornish Labour News*, 56 (May 1937).
33. John Legonna (c. 1976), unpublished autobiographical manuscript, Institute of Cornish Studies (University of Exeter).
34. *New Cornwall*, Vol. 11, 2 (March 1963).
35. Legonna, unpublished autobiographical manuscript.
36. Interview with Cecil Beer, 25 November 1996, CAVA.
37. Beer, 25 November 1996, CAVA.

III

MK – THE FORMATIVE YEARS: 1940–60

The creation of Mebyon Kernow in 1951 was symbolic of the changing nature of Cornish nationalism during the middle decades of the twentieth century. From the early 1940s onwards there was a greater acceptance of the need to focus on the interests of contemporary Cornwall, which was evident in the wartime activities of the proto-nationalist Young Cornwall movement and a general trend towards anti-metropolitanism by the late 1940s. Indeed, at a time of renewed public interest in the condition of Cornwall and the other Celtic nations there was a unique opportunity for the politicisation of the Revivalist movement to finally take place. MK embraced the role of a political pressure group and placed a series of constitutional and socio-economic issues relating to Cornwall on the public agenda. But beneath the surface there was still uncertainty over the future direction of the Cornish movement, with the strands of cultural and political nationalism not yet entwined. By the mid-1950s a combination of personal and ideological differences had really brought the formative phase of the movement to a close. The latter part of the decade witnessed a retreat from political radicalism as MK struggled to remain a united and relevant force.

The 'Pre-MK atmosphere': 1940–50

A critical factor in the wartime development of Cornish nationalism was the growing recognition by new activists of the need for a political agenda. Oral history is particularly relevant for studying this period. Apart from the relative absence of written sources of information, we are essentially talking about the unrecorded activities of a small number of individuals. One such person was Richard Jenkin (see Appendix). His life history provides a useful introduction to, what he describes as, the 'Pre-MK atmosphere'. Born in Manchester in October 1925, Richard Garfield Jenkin was the son of a Mousehole man who, like so many young Cornish people then and now, had to leave Cornwall to find work, eventually becoming a clergyman. During his teenage years Richard Jenkin made frequent visits to Manchester Central Library and 'amongst other things would look at anything about Cornwall and Cornish'. As the following oral narrative extract suggests, at this stage Jenkin's interest in the history and culture of Cornwall was pursued on an individual and isolated basis:

> And this was wartime now and this is where I first came across the Cornish miracle plays, in Manchester Central Library. I used to try and look at that, though I couldn't do much with it. I recognised some words, that was about all ... I got hold of a bookseller's catalogue ... and found the only book which seemed to refer to Cornish at all, apart from travel books and guides ... was a book by 'Halwyn' (R St. V Allin-Collins), *A Supplement to the Cornish Grammar and some Short Stories*. So I sent off for this, I was about fourteen or fifteen then ... I got it and the other thing I got more or less at the same time was a copy of Carew's *Survey of Cornwall*, which I bought from a Manchester bookshop in the wartime. And I read that from cover to cover to find out everything I could about Cornwall ... I hadn't even heard of the Gorseth. I didn't even know it existed; it was purely self-education! Well, then I went to Oxford for a year, before I went into the army. And at Oxford for the first time I met other people who were interested in Cornish.[1]

This encounter with other young Cornishmen and women at university presented Richard Jenkin with an opportunity to display, articulate and develop his 'Cornishness'. The outbreak of war had reduced the activities of the mainstream Revivalist organisations to a bare minimum. Gorseth Kernow was held in the form of a 'closed' ceremony at the Royal Institution of Cornwall in Truro, while Tyr ha Tavas was effectively dormant and now only existed in the form of a Cornish writing circle, the Scoren Kescryfa Kernewek. Given these circumstances Jenkin and his student associates, including John Legonna who was now studying at Oxford under A.L. Rowse, decided in 1943 to form a new patriotic organisation. Entitled the Young Cornwall Movement, it was based on the inspiration of Guiseppe Mazzini's Young Italy. Although accepting the goal of self-government, it was significant that Young Cornwall 'didn't make it a great issue' because it wanted to attract wider support from Cornish university students. Jenkin's personal memories of this period offer us a rare glimpse into the aims and activities of the group:

> I met some people who were actually interested in Cornish and

we set up a little organisation. (It was intended to be a big organisation but it never grew!): the Young Cornwall Movement ... It intended to take political stances about the problems of Cornwall as well as learning the language and becoming full Cornish citizens ... There was David Balhatchet from Porthcothan near Padstow ... There was his girlfriend Mary Foss from Penzance (they eventually married), and there was John Legonna ... The Young Cornwall Movement was intended to be an organisation of Cornish students and they picked up one or two from other Universities eventually, but communications during wartime were difficult and it finally faded out.[2]

This desire for a movement that could raise contemporary Cornish issues was not restricted to the members of Young Cornwall. George Pawley White, who was to become the first treasurer of MK, served in India during the war. He remembers writing in Cornish to Robert Morton Nance and 'suggesting ... that it was time that we formed some national gathering. I didn't say political party or anything like that but I thought the time was coming when we ought to be drawn together and make a united front for Cornwall'. Yet it appears that he received a rather cool response from the Grand Bard. Pawley White recalls that Nance 'was always very cagey on the idea: he didn't like going into politics. He was very much more for the literary side and historical side rather than the practical political side'.[3] Despite this reluctance, the end of the war provided the key founders of MK with an opportunity to play a more active role in Cornish affairs. As Pawley White recalled, 'I think probably a number of us had been away from Cornwall, just as I had been out in India all those years, and began to realise how much Cornwall meant to us. And how easy it would be for it to pass into history if we didn't do something about it'.[4] Helena Charles (see Appendix) expressed a similar view. A graduate of Oxford University, she had returned to Redruth in 1948 and by the following year had become the Cornish representative on the Central Committee of European Communities and Regions. The development of her ideas was evident in an article in the *Cornish Review* in 1949 when she warned of the threat to the Cornish identity:

Breton reaction to French persecution and repression has been a vigorous revival of Breton culture, and large numbers of French-speaking Bretons have learnt their language. Unless Cornish people react with equal vigour to the process of assimilation to England that is taking place, we shall become just another English county, and it will be left to our daughter nation to safeguard our Celtic heritage, which we are rapidly betraying.[5]

The events surrounding the 1950 Celtic Congress, which was held that year in Truro at the Royal Institution of Cornwall, gave a further boost to the embryonic nationalist movement. A Celtic Congress should have been held in Truro in 1939 but the outbreak of the Second World War had meant its cancellation. Newspaper reports reveal that large delegations from both Brittany and Wales would have been in attendance if this event had gone ahead and it is an interesting point of conjecture whether this would have led to an earlier politicisation of the Cornish movement.[6] For Pawley White the period leading up to the 1950 Congress was significant since it brought together individuals like Lambert Truran, Ernest Retallack Hooper and Charles Thomas, particularly during the rehearsals for Bewnans Meriasek which was performed at the Congress in Cornish. Jenkin also points out that 'people were beginning to ... make contact with other people, finding that they had the same sort of ideas. But if you had been on your own for years and you were a nationalist in spirit then you suddenly found half a dozen people with similar ideas. You get together and then you feel you can do something'. This was particularly the case since contacts were also made with individuals from the other Celtic nations:

> I was able to ... meet all of the leading figures of the Cornish movement of the time ... some who became leading figures later on, and people from other Celtic countries. I've got a photograph somewhere of that congress with Morton Nance and Cynan who was then the Arch Druid of Wales in the front and Professor Ambrose Bebb in the front and I was there in the back! And so was Lambert Truran, and Martin Yelland who died quite young actually and people I still know in Wales like Delwyn Philips and Eibhlin Ni Chathailriabhaigh from Ireland and so on. They are all there and so I have known them since 1950 onwards! ... It was through the Celtic Congress that I met Helena Charles and her band of actors who performed Bewnans Meriasek ... From that we found a lot of people who were of the same mind, about the problems of Cornwall and the culture of Cornwall and so on. It was from that that Mebyon Kernow was founded in 1951.[7]

This exchange of ideas must be seen against the background of wider political, cultural and economic developments in the immediate post-war period. Events elsewhere in the Celtic world, such as the Scottish Covenant campaign in 1948 which collected nearly two million signatures in support of a Scottish Parliament, suggested a renewed public interest in the nationalist cause. This encouraged the younger generation of Celtic Revivalists in Cornwall to move in a political direction. Although the cultural dimension was still an instinctive vehicle for expressing Cornish

nationalist views, it appears that the nature of culturalism was now changing from a passive, antiquarian attitude to a passionate concern over the
perceived threat to Cornish identity. The Horler debate in 1949 is a good
example. In the summer edition of *Cornish Review* the detective writer,
Sydney Horler who lived at Bude in North Cornwall, launched a public
attack on the character of the Cornish people. Castigating the local population for their 'farmyard immorality', which Horler appeared to suggest
was the product of the supremacy of Cornish Methodism, he expressed
his refusal 'to have anything to do with the "locals"'. The hysterical
nature of his attack can be seen in the following extract from his rather
lengthy letter to the journal:

> What is the reason for this deplorable anti-social behaviour?
> The principal cause, I believe, is that the Cornish, a primitive
> people at the best, cut off for centuries from the rest of the coun-
> try, have always hated the intrusion of anyone from outside –
> the 'foreigner', as they call him. They like his money, but they
> keenly resent his physical presence. And the kinder and more
> generous he is on arrival, the more they will hate and fleece him.
> This is the stark truth. Perhaps being a very backward, illiterate
> and ignorant people, they develop a strong sense of inferiority
> when they come into contact with anyone of a different and bet-
> ter type; but the fact remains that the 'foreigner' is only safe if
> he leaves them strictly alone.[8]

Not surprisingly, Horler's comments produced a furious reaction from readers in the subsequent issue. This included nationalist activists like Helena
Charles and Cyril Curnow, with the latter remarking 'It is our individuality
that they dislike. Probably they fear a nationalist party in Cornwall'.[9] For
Jenkin this incident was significant in the formulation of nationalist sentiment since it 'gave us a kick-start in effect'. It was a view that he also
emphasised in his pamphlet *40 Years of Mebyon Kernow*, in which he
appeared to give symbolic importance to the debate at a time when 'Cornish nationality needed to be expressed in every department of life if it was
not to succumb to the ever increasing pressure of modern centralism'.[10] As
the events of the early 1950s were to demonstrate, such sentiments were to
influence the ideological direction of MK as it in turn attempted to influence public opinion in Cornwall during its formative years.

In addition, the emergence of MK took place at a time when there
was a growing public debate over economic conditions in Cornwall. In
1947 the University College of the South West (later renamed as the
University of Exeter) published a survey of conditions in Cornwall and
Devon. The survey committee found that a number of areas, notably

the Cornwall-Devon borderland and the far west, suffered from limited vocational opportunities, relatively high unemployment and out-migration. A more balanced industrial structure was required in order to 'counteract' the tendency for younger members of the community to leave rural areas in search of better employment opportunities and it was further proposed that there should be an improvement in housing conditions and rural amenities.[11] The political and cultural dimensions of these underlying economic difficulties were addressed in an editorial in the *Cornish Review* in the autumn of 1949. It was claimed that 'inept Government restrictions' were undermining the potential of Cornwall's staple industries, notably fishing, mining and farming. By focusing on the interests of these core economic concerns, combined with recognition of the crucial relationship between culture and economic regeneration, an economic strategy for Cornwall could be developed.[12]

Yet, with hindsight, the immediate post-war years can also be seen as something of a mini-economic boom period. New industrial estates in the Camborne-Redruth area and, in comparison with the 1930s, relatively full employment had actually helped to reverse the chronic population outflow that Cornwall had experienced almost continuously since the 1870s. Perhaps these more expansive economic conditions were a more favourable context for the leap into organised political nationalism, as this small group of concerned Cornish people, which included several professionals and teachers, began to feel the need to ensure that post-war economic development retained a Cornish dimension. Indicative of this period was the formation in 1950 of the short-lived Cornish Independence Party with a programme that strongly emphasised the need for economic regeneration.[13] This growing interest in the affairs of Cornwall was also evident in contemporary political debates at that time. The Conservatives, now in opposition following the Labour landslide of 1945, claimed that they would be more successful than the other two parties in managing economic progress and developing the rural infrastructure of the region. In 1950, Conservative candidates in Cornwall were actually criticised by some of their opponents for being 'more concerned with the welfare of their own constituencies than with the wider and more important national and international issues'.[14] This public interest in local issues was to provide the context for MK's own attempts to develop an economic strategy in the early 1950s.

'A Square Deal for the Cornish': 1951–56

A series of meetings after the 1950 Congress paved the way for the creation of MK. It appears that Professor Ambrose Bebb, a leading figure in Plaid Cymru, played an influential role in the emergence of the new movement. Jenkin recounts that Bebb was 'staying with Charles Thomas's family. After the Congress was over he came and visited me at home up in St. Mewan, to discuss how Plaid Cymru had started and to encourage us to go on and to do the same'.[15] The official launch of MK took place at Oates' Temperance Hotel in Redruth on Saturday 6th January 1951. It was agreed that membership was to 'be open to all Cornish people every-where', a reminder of the movement's ethnic nationalism at this point, on the understanding that they were initially proposed and seconded by committee members. The committee itself consisted of Helena Charles (chairman), Lambert Truran (secretary), George Pawley White (treasurer) and four ordinary members (E.G. Retallack Hooper, Charles Thomas, Martin Yelland and John Davey). Other founder members of what was described as this 'forward-looking patriotic society' included Richard Jenkin, Ann Trevenen, Bertha Hooper and Francis Cargeeg. The society's logo was to incorporate the cross of St. Piran and members agreed to investigate a number of contemporary issues, such as the effect of imports on the Cornish economy and the future prospects of the mining industry. This historic meeting also agreed to accept an earlier suggestion of seven core aims for MK:

1. To study local conditions and attempt to remedy any that may be prejudicial to the best interests of Cornwall by the creation of public opinion or other appropriate means.

2. To foster the Cornish language and literature.

3. To encourage the study of Cornish history from a Cornish point of view.

4. By self-knowledge, to further the acceptance of the idea of the Celtic character of Cornwall, one of the six Celtic nations.

5. To publish pamphlets, broadsheets, articles and letters in the Press whenever possible, putting forward the foregoing aims.

6. To arrange concerts and entertainments with a Cornish Celtic flavour through which these aims can be further advanced.

7. To co-operate with all societies concerned with preserving the character of Cornwall.[16]

These aims were remarkably similar to the agenda of Tyr ha Tavas back in the 1930s. No specific reference was made at this stage to the political issue of Home Rule and it was not until September 1951 that clause 4 was replaced with the phrase 'To further the acceptance of the Celtic character of Cornwall and its right to self-government in domestic af-fairs in a Federated United Kingdom'.[17] This point suggests that culturalism was still a priority for the founder members of the group.

Even Helena Charles, a leading advocate of the need for MK to embrace constitutional reform, played an active role in the cultural side of the Revival. She was responsible for arranging the performance of Bewnans Meryasek at Perran Round in July 1951 by Gwaryoryon Gernewek, a group affiliated to MK. Two years later Charles was initiated as a language bard at Trethevy Quoit, while MK itself pursued a range of cultural activities during its formative years, from the regular production of Cornish calendars to sending a birthday prayer in Cornish to the Duke of Cornwall.[18]

Despite this initial impression of cultural conservatism, it is evident that the leadership of MK was committed to constitutional objectives from the very beginning. A discussion document apparently circulated by Charles before the foundation of the society emphasised the need for Cornwall to take its rightful place in a federal Britain. Although Charles expressed her agreement 'with much that had been said about the need for caution and prudence', she argued that the 'process of anglicisation and assimilation [was] proceeding fast'. The *Survey of Devon and Cornwall* in 1947, she added, had painted 'a grim picture of the decline in the population except in those areas where retired Anglo-Saxons are settling because they want a warm … climate to die in, or where the tourist industry is spreading. These population trends, coupled with the centralisation that is only a little less than in France, will result in a few generations in the *disappearance* of the Cornish'. This threat to Cornish identity was too serious and immediate 'for any purely theoretic idea of nationhood and language to have any chance of succeeding'. Adopting a Poujadist concern for the interests of the *petite bourgeoisie*, it was claimed that MK needed to forge an alliance of 'small tradesmen, farmers, etc., who are tired of being pushed around by Whitehall'.[19]

Another feature of the early MK was its emphasis on the need for greater career opportunities in Cornwall. It was claimed that the vast majority of the growing number of public sector jobs, particularly in education and local government, were deliberately being denied to local people, a factor that further exacerbated the traditional problem of out-migration by younger members of the community. For MK this process was undermining Cornish culture. A press statement by the society claimed that the 'most glaring example' of anglicisation was 'County Hall, which is staffed almost entirely in the upper grades by people from up the country. Nearly all the Heads of senior and county schools are not Cornish; six of the eight Deputy Lord Lieutenants of Cornwall are not Cornish; the Chief Constable is not Cornish … Only one member of Parliament [Harold Hayman, Labour MP for Falmouth-Camborne] is Cornish!'.[20] This concern over the cultural impact of in-migration was

also publicly expressed by a leading figure in the Cornish labour movement. In 1953 George Thomas, secretary of the Penzance Trades Council, caused considerable controversy when he publicly declared that
the Cornish were in danger of being 'pushed off Lands End' by new
residents from across the Tamar:

> For some years I have noticed that persons from other parts of
> the British Isles were taking the most lucrative appointments in
> Cornwall. In Local Government, in Teaching, in the nationalised
> industries, all the best jobs were going to foreigners … I want
> Cornwall to remain Cornish, that our Celtic strain shall be pre-
> served, that those coming to our Country from other parts shall
> not change Cornwall from its Cornishness. As one of Cornwall's
> leading Trade Unionists I claim to speak for the vast majority of
> our working people.[21]

The nationalist challenge of MK was promoted from 1952 onwards by
New Cornwall. Although this was technically an independent monthly
publication, it was edited and distributed by leading members of the
new society. The first ten issues were actually edited by Richard
Gendall, under the pseudonym 'R. Morris', and then by Helena Charles
until her resignation from the post of MK chairman in 1956. From the
start *New Cornwall* pursued a radical editorial policy, combining fea-
tures on devolution with socio-economic issues. Home Rule was not
advocated on purely romantic or historical grounds since Charles
saw Cornish nationalism as a way of challenging the inherent 'apathy
and laziness in local affairs' that had prevailed 'for a great many years'.
Only a 'colossal effort to achieve self-government in domestic affairs
would bring about the regeneration of Cornish people necessary to
take away this reproach'.[22] The group was particularly critical of those
economy-minded councillors whose sole purpose in local government was 'to keep the rates down'. MK believed that this mentality
was undermining vital areas of Cornish life, particularly in education
where it was pointed out that expenditure by the County Council was
low compared to other authorities.[23] In 1953 this critical attitude towards local government led Charles to contest a by-election for a seat
on Camborne-Redruth Urban District Council. Using the slogan, 'A
Square Deal for the Cornish', her manifesto emphasised the need for
regional self-government and called on local government to tackle
social issues like unemployment and poor housing conditions. The
eventual result was encouraging. Although there was a low turnout
of just 11 per cent, Charles emerged victorious with 77.6 per cent of
the vote in a straight fight with Labour.

Mebyon Kernow's ideas enjoyed a somewhat mixed reception from the political establishment. By the early 1950s the Conservatives were starting to move away from the neo-liberal stance which they had previously adopted in response to the Attlee administrations, though a debate on Home Rule organised by the Truro Young Conservatives and the pro-decentralisation comments of a local Conservative representative on a BBC 'Any Questions' programme from Liskeard in 1952 indicated some interest.[24] Labour activists tended to be opposed on principle to the concept of devolution. Despite the personal comments of George Thomas on inmigration, the main emphasis of the Cornish Labour movement was now on state socialism rather than the community socialism that had been articulated by A.L. Rowse and others during the inter-war period. In 1952 the Labour candidate for Bodmin dismissed the idea of Cornish Home Rule as unnecessary and a 'backward step'. This view was echoed by Michael Foot, MP for Plymouth Devonport, who declared that 'the Welsh and the Cornish are far too sensible to want their own parliaments'.[25] Even Hayman, who was regarded as generally sympathetic to the Cornish movement, seemed unwilling to endorse the core political demand of a regional assembly.[26]

The Liberals, however, were willing to embrace the anti-metropolitan cause in Cornwall. Regionalism offered the party a distinctive political role at a time when it was struggling to survive in the aftermath of its disastrous performance in the 1951 general election when even in Cornwall it had been relegated to third place. During the early 1950s the party started to exploit the economic grievances of rural voters, presenting themselves as the champions of local interest groups and claiming that Cornwall would be 'far better served' by MPs who were independent of the 'Tory and Socialist machines' in London.[27] Some Liberals accepted the constitutional objectives of the Cornish movement. In May 1952 John Foot, a son of Isaac, and Stuart Roseveare, prospective candidate for Bodmin, expressed their support for local Home Rule on the grounds that the 'Cornish people were a separate nation'. A representative from party headquarters in London even indicated that Cornwall could have total control over its own domestic affairs with just defence and foreign policy remaining with Westminster.[28] There was a belief on the part of some MK activists that closer links with the Liberals could advance their cause. Richard Jenkin pointed to Scotland where support from the SNP had helped the Liberals to increase their share of the vote at the Inverness by-election in December 1954. He added that 'we cannot agree that any kind of devolution or home rule would be possible under a Labour government, since socialism is *per se*, centralisation, and if it ceased to be centralising would no longer be socialism. On the other hand, the Liberal Party is pledged to parliaments for Wales and Scotland'.[29]

Yet there was growing concern within the wider Cornish movement over the new emphasis on political objectives. Prominent individuals like Edmund Hambly, former leader of Tyr ha Tavas, publicly expressed their concern over what they saw as the 'separatist' agenda of MK. In response Charles and her supporters seemed at times to be critical of what they described as the 'passive and antiquarian attitude' of the Revivalist establishment. This situation was viewed with alarm by Robert Morton Nance, Grand Bard of the Cornish Gorseth until his death in 1959. He believed that the radical image of MK might alienate the purely cultural wing, symbolised by the Gorseth and the Old Cornwall Societies, and adopted a 'cautiously non-committal attitude' throughout the decade.[30] References to a 'possible New Cornwall-Old Cornwall showdown' during the Charles era were reminiscent of the pre-war tensions between the Gorseth and Tyr ha Tavas, which reflected the inherent reluctance of the mainstream Cornish movement to move away radically from its antiquarian origins some fifty years earlier. Even founder members of Mebyon Kernow like Charles Thomas and Retallack Hooper (Talek), who ironically had been in favour of a political agenda for Tyr ha Tavas back in the 1930s, were increasingly disenchanted with the aims of the group. Their hostile attitude to the strident nationalism of Helena Charles can clearly be seen in the following extract from a letter written by Thomas to Morton Nance in 1954:

> … we have got progressively less interested since Miss Charles announced her agenda in this order, Home Rule, Support for Scottish Home Rule, Support for Welsh Home Rule, Support for imprisoned Breton leaders, and now membership of this Congress of Minorities, which means asking her MK members to finance her jaunts to the continent. Neither Talek or I have been to a meeting for 18 months or so, and I am afraid what started as a genuine effort to preserve Cornish culture has become a political platform.[31]

Charles herself was increasingly frustrated by what she regarded as the 'total apathy' of MK activists. Oral testimonies from founder members create an image of a 'dynamic [but] difficult' person whose eccentric personality was likely to cause friction within the group. Pawley White remembers that towards the end of her period as leader she had concluded that 'there was nothing worth saving in Cornwall except the scenery'.[32] MK's 'scattered membership' meant that meetings were poorly attended and nearly half of the subscriptions for 1955 were not paid. Charles was particularly disillusioned when she lost her St. Day seat on Camborne-Redruth UDC in the 1955 council elections. Despite campaigning on a

Mebyon Kernow platform, she complained that 'no one with any Cornish nationalist leanings was sufficiently interested to work for me, but the Labour Party [represented by 'an unknown upcountryman'] had plenty of canvassers and drivers'.[33] The lack of direction in MK was confirmed in February 1957, a few months after the resignation of Charles, when a commissioned report was published on the financial implications of Cornish devolution. The writer, an economics graduate from the University of Wales, had been asked by Charles to explore the subject in detail. Yet his report was seriously flawed by an assumption that a federal devolution of power meant the same thing as complete independence. Not surprisingly the report, which was widely publicised in newspapers like the *Western Morning News*, concluded that the 'plea for Cornish independence' was simply not practical.[34] It was an incident that also demonstrated that MK was not even operating as an effective pressure group for Cornish nationalism.

The Beer Years: 1957–60

Following the resignation of Charles the divided nationalist movement had to look for a new leader. Perhaps as a sign of MK's despair, some members now approached Major Cecil Beer, a former civil servant and pre-war Revivalist who was not even a member of the group, and invited him to become chairman. It was ironic that Beer, who had served as secretary for Tyr ha Tavas, had actually been instrumental in opposing the politicisation of the Cornish movement in the 1930s on the grounds that it was essential to concentrate on developing the cultural infrastructure of the Revival. Now he accepted the case for some form of devolution and agreed to become chairman of MK on condition that it was only on a temporary basis. Beer's position on the future direction of Mebyon Kernow was in total contrast to that of Charles. He believed that the main priority was to keep the group together and claimed that the 'rather determined views' of Charles had caused unnecessary friction with other Cornish organisations. Echoing Morton Nance's call for unity he expressed his desire that 'all branches of the Cornish movement should keep in harmony with one another, in tolerance of each others opinions, having but one ultimate aim, – unity and the preservation of our Cornish Nationhood'.[35] Beer's comments in an interview in 1996 indicate his long-held belief that the task of winning the public argument for Cornwall's right to an Assembly would be a slow and uphill struggle. Yet as the movement grew, with 'more supporting angles', it was also inevitable that the idea that Cornwall was historically not part of England would eventually lead to a wider acceptance of the right of the

Cornish to some form of self-government. Rejecting the radical stance of Charles, or for that matter the electoral politics of recent decades, Beer showed that he was more comfortable with the campaign group role inherited from Tyr ha Tavas:

> I was sympathetic to the general cause, as it was then. They hadn't such an election manifesto as they have now. It was simpler, it was more ... a ginger group to ... write to MPs and other influential people to try and get something done more for Cornwall.[36]

This 'simpler' approach at least provided MK with an opportunity to recover from the divisions of its formative years. Jenkin describes the three years under Beer's leadership as a time of 'quiet but steady' growth for Mebyon Kernow. Beer's achievement, he added, was to make MK an organisation which 'ordinary Cornish people could take an interest in. I mean if you go too far too soon ordinary people are going to think you are crazy'.[37] In that sense the late 1950s witnessed the start of a process that was to culminate in the brief popularity of MK in the subsequent decade. By 1958 the return to Cornwall of several activists formerly living in England meant that the group was 'again expanding, with new members and new spheres of activity'. Beer's election as chairman was accompanied by the creation of a fresh committee, while an attempt was made at creating local branches, notably in the Penryn-Falmouth area.[38] In addition, Richard and Ann Jenkin took over from Charles as editors of *New Cornwall*. As Richard Jenkin suggests, they also introduced a new approach to nationalism, moving away from the concentration on pure politics to a broader appeal to the wider cultural movement:

> We changed it from being a MK (more or less) internal magazine, to making it, or trying to make it, the magazine for the whole Cornish movement. And somewhere in it I wrote, 'New Cornwall is accused of being the Mebyon Kernow magazine. It's not the Mebyon Kernow magazine anymore than it is the RIC magazine or the Cornwall archaeological magazine or any other society I belong to'. We wanted to cover the whole aspect of Cornish culture and development.[39]

An article in *New Cornwall* on the tenth anniversary of the birth of MK even appeared to downplay the constitutional dimension. It was stressed by 'a founder member' of the movement that in 'its ten years of life it had fought indefatigably for its main aim:- to remind Cornish people of their unique culture and to develop it in every way and by every means'. The issue of self-government was only mentioned briefly towards the end of the article. Even then devolution was advocated more on cultural than economic grounds, with the writer concluding that constitutional reform was essential to 'maintain the Cornishness of Cornwall and to encourage Cornish people to be proud of their country and their heritage'.[40] Yet on reflection this focus on culturalism was not really surprising. After all, many of the present-day icons of Cornishness were only starting to be accepted at that time. In 1953 it was reported by *New Cornwall* that opinions still differed as to whether St. Petroc, St. Michael or St. Piran was the true patron saint of Cornwall. It was suggested as a compromise 'that readers do all that they can to honour all three'.[41] The public adoption of the St. Piran's cross as the national flag of Cornwall also dates from this period. In the early 1950s MK had campaigned vigorously for greater recognition of this emblem and the movement was encouraged by reports of its adoption at different places throughout Cornwall, particularly at the 1953 Coronation. Yet even at the end of the decade, it was evident that the movement was still not united over this basic cultural symbol, with some activists calling for a more colourful flag design to replace the black and white cross of St. Piran.[42] Such a debate shows how the activities of MK were central to the creation of at least one contemporary symbol of Cornish identity.

On the negative side, however, the subsequent combination of cultural and political activities also prevented MK from developing into an effective force. Since committee meetings covered such a wide variety of topics, ranging from boundary disputes with Devon to the production of bilingual paper serviettes, it was difficult to establish a clear sense of direction for the group.[43] In these circumstances it is tempting to regard the late 1950s as a low point in the evolution of Cornish nationalism. Yet to fully understand this period we need to go beyond MK to look at the wider politics of Revivalism. Indeed, while the nationalist movement itself was struggling to adopt a forward-looking agenda in the aftermath of Charles' resignation, a new personality had emerged on the Cornish political scene. In December 1956 Peter Bessell was invited to contest the Bodmin constituency for the Liberal Party following Stuart Roseveare's retirement on the grounds of ill health. The business background of the new Liberal candidate encouraged him to take a close interest in the economic problems of Cornwall. At a time when Harold Macmillan, the British Prime Minister, was declaring that 'most of our people have never had it so good', Cornwall was still experiencing relatively high unemployment and low wages. Bessell based his campaign strategy around such issues, producing a monthly magazine entitled *Spotlight on Cornwall* and calling for urgent action to develop the local economy.[44]

This consideration of economic issues led Bessell to take on the

practical task of developing the Liberal Party's anti-metropolitan identity in Cornwall. Although he was not a member of MK at that time, he
instinctively recognised the need for separate regional status for Cornwall. His initial interest in the subject appears to have emerged out of
ideas for developing the local tourist industry through attracting visitors from overseas. On a visit to the United States in 1958 Bessell was
surprised to receive very little information on Cornwall when he asked
for tourist details from the British Information Service. He believed that
this reflected the 'failure of Cornwall to establish itself as a separate
country'. The only way to attract wealthy tourists, particularly from
overseas, was to copy the example of the other Celtic nations and use
cultural identity as a marketing device to overcome the London-orientated tourist information services. A campaign to preserve and promote the distinctive Celtic culture of the area was now needed to achieve
this objective:

> The Welsh and the Scots rightly take a great pride in the histori-
> cal and cultural traditions of their countries. Cornwall has an
> equal claim to distinction historically. The virtual death of the
> Cornish language is a tragedy. I believe a great drive is needed
> during the next decade to re-establish Cornwall's claim to be
> recognised as a part of the British Isles, with a distinctive his-
> tory, culture, language and traditions. It is not only a matter of
> self-regard and Cornish pride; it is also a matter of sound com-
> mercial common sense.[45]

He then proceeded to develop a five-point plan for raising the profile of
heritage tourism. Apart from making a number of practical suggestions,
including the idea that Bodmin Moor should be developed as an Ameri-
can-style National Park, Bessell appealed once again for a 'real drive to
develop Cornwall as a country apart, rather than as just a county'. The
term 'Royal Duchy of Cornwall', along with the area's 'Celtic ancestry',
needed to be promoted in order to attract overseas visitors. Central to
this strategy would be an Annual National Festival of Cornwall covering
the Cornish language and local artistic events, which could eventually
rival the Edinburgh Festival and the International Eisteddfod at
Llangollen.[46] It has been pointed out, however, that Bessell 'was a
minority voice in a predominately anti-tourist Cornish movement'.[47] A
copy of the plan did appear in *New Cornwall*, which suggests that
there was some interest in the proposals from its editors. Nevertheless,
in the following edition Bessell's plan was criticised by a reader of the
journal on the grounds that the area needed to be protected from over-
development. He added that tourism was 'only a side-line for men's

wives to earn a few extra shillings serving in cafes or washing dishes; it holds nothing whatsoever for the man of the house, or the son who wants steady work'.[48]

This criticism was somewhat unfair since Bessell was also concerned with the threat of over-development. As he stressed in his plan, Cornwall's 'delightful beauty spots and untouched villages must not be sacrificed to an unrestrained tide of commercialism'. An imaginative focus on the theme of Celtic culture might have offered both an alternative to conventional tourism and a practical way of meeting the aspirations of the post-war Revivalists. Besides, for Bessell tourism formed just part of a wider strategy designed to encourage local initiative throughout the Duchy. He argued that in strategic terms the Cornish economy could only be expanded by a concentration on the three sectors of agriculture, mining (including china clay) and tourism. Light industry from outside should only be encouraged to those areas where its 'presence would not affect the natural beauty of the Duchy'.[49] By 1959 he had even formed a non-profit making company, Cornish Development Ltd, to encourage a self-sufficient and locally based economy.

Significantly, this regional economic plan was to be linked to political devolution. An early indication of Bessell's support for constitutional reform came in August 1958 at the same time that he was developing his scheme for marketing Cornwall's heritage. Whilst rejecting the slogan 'Home Rule for Cornwall', which he interpreted at that stage to mean complete autonomy, he stressed the need for the region to be given a 'measure of devolution' in line with Liberal proposals for the other Celtic nations. This theme was developed a few days later in a speech at Kelly Bray when he declared that the 'problems of Cornwall are so many and so distinctive that the only way Parliament can effectively deal with them is by giving the MPs for the Duchy special powers to legislate in local matters'.[50] In response to a questionnaire issued to parliamentary candidates by MK at the 1959 general election, Bessell accepted the case for a regional assembly and added that devolution should be considered as 'vital' for the economic development of Cornwall. Bessell's party colleagues supported him, especially Gerald Whitmarsh, the candidate for St. Ives, who placed 'Cornwall in a similar category to Wales'. Whilst the Conservative and Labour candidates, including Hayman, were lukewarm or even hostile, *New Cornwall* concluded that the five Liberals 'all desire more real devolution'.[51] This surrogate nationalist stance of Cornish Liberalism was even more significant given the results of the 1959 election. Although Cornwall's parliamentary representation did not alter for the third election in a row, with the Conservatives still on four seats and Labour with one, the Liberals were able to increase their share of the vote at the expense of the other parties and move back into second place behind the Conservatives. The significance of this result was that the political ideas initially raised by MK at the start of the decade were now being championed by the new rising force in Cornish politics.

Notes

1. Interview with Richard Jenkin, 14 February 2000, Cornish Audio Visual Archive (CAVA).
2. Jenkin, 14 February 2000, CAVA.
3. Interview with George Pawley White, 25 January 2000, CAVA.
4. Pawley White, 14 September 2001, CAVA.
5. *Cornish Review*, 3 (Autumn 1949), p. 38.
6. *Western Morning News*, 6 September 1939.
7. Pawley White, 14 September 2001, CAVA; Jenkin, 3 October 2001, CAVA.
8. *Cornish Review, 2* (Summer 1949), pp. 99–100.
9. *Cornish Review, 3* (Autumn 1949), p. 104.
10. Jenkin, 3 October 2001, CAVA; Richard Jenkin (1991), *40 Years of Mebyon Kernow*, Leedstown, p. 1.
11. University College of the South West (1947), *Devon and Cornwall – A Preliminary Survey*, Exeter, pp. 13–34.
12. *Cornish Review, 3* (Autumn 1949), 3, pp. 15–18.
13. *Western Morning News*, April 1950.
14. *Cornish Guardian*, 16 May 1946; *Western Morning News*, 9, 19 and 23 February 1950.
15. Jenkin, 3 October 2001, CAVA.
16. Agenda and notes for the inaugural meeting of Mebyon Kernow, 6 January 1951, MK Collection. The following chapters lean heavily on the minutes of MK general and National Executive Committee meetings plus letters to and from MK officers and other material. There are collections of such MK material at the Institute of Cornish Studies, Truro and at the Cornwall Record Office, where they are in the process of being catalogued.
17. Jenkin, *40 Years of Mebyon Kernow*, pp. 2–3.
18. *New Cornwall*, Vol. 5, 1 (December 1956-January 1957).
19. Unpublished discussion document presented to the inaugural meeting of Mebyon Kernow, 6 January 1951, MK Collection.
20. Undated press statement from the early 1950s, MK Collection.
21. *New Cornwall*, 7 (April 1953).
22. *New Cornwall*, 1 (October 1952); *New Cornwall* (c. February 1956), MK Collection.
23. *New Cornwall*, (c. February 1956), MK Collection.
24. *New Cornwall*, Vol. 3, 5 (March 1955); *Cornish Guardian*, 8 May 1952.
25. *Cornish Guardian*, 8 May 1952; *New Cornwall*, 11 (August 1953).
26. *New Cornwall*, Vol. 7, 6 (October-November 1959), pp. 8–9.
27. For a discussion of this subject see Garry Tregidga (2000), *The Liberal Party in South-West Britain since 1918: Political Decline, Dormancy and Rebirth*, Exeter, pp. 158–62.
28. *Cornish Guardian*, 8 May 1952.
29. *New Cornwall*, Vol. 2, 6 (April 1954); *New Cornwall* (c. December 1955), MK Collection.

30. Undated newspaper cuttings from the early 1950s, MK Collection; *New Cornwall*, Vol. 7, 5 (August-September 1959).
31. Letter from Charles Thomas to Robert Morton Nance, 18 October 1954, MK Collection.
32. Pawley White, 14 September 2001, CAVA.
33. MK committee minutes, 12 August 1955; undated memorandum from Helena Charles to MK members, c. 1956, MK Collection.
34. *Western Morning News*, 3 May 1957.
35. Interview with Cecil Beer, 25 November 1996, CAVA; *New Cornwall*, Vol. 7, 5 (August-September 1959).
36. Interview with Beer, 25 November 1996, CAVA.
37. Jenkin, *40 Years of Mebyon Kernow*, p. 4; Jenkin, 3 October 2001, CAVA.
38. *New Cornwall*, Vol. 5, 2 (February-March 1957); *New Cornwall*, Vol. 6, 6 (October-November 1958); *Falmouth Packet*, 2 October 1959.
39. Jenkin, 3 October 2001, CAVA.
40. *New Cornwall*, Vol. 9, 1 (December 1960–January 1961).
41. *New Cornwall*, 9 (June 1953).
42. *New Cornwall*, Vol. 8, 3 (April-May 1960); minutes of MK meeting, 8 October 1960, MK Collection.
43. Minutes of MK meeting, 8 October 1960, MK Collection.
44. *Cornish Guardian*, 8 August 1957; *Cornish Times*, 31 January 1958.
45. *Cornish Times*, 15 August 1958.
46. The 1959 election address of Peter Bessell, DM 668, National Liberal Club Collection, University of Bristol.
47. Ronald Perry (1999), 'The Changing Face of Celtic Tourism in Cornwall, 1875–1975', *Cornish Studies: Seven*, Exeter, p. 104.
48. *New Cornwall*, Vol. 8, 4, (June-July 1960).
49. *Cornish Times*, 31 January 1958.
50. *Cornish Times*, 15 and 22 August 1958.
51. *New Cornwall*, Vol. 7, 6 (October-November 1959).

IV

LOOKING FOR VOTES: 1960–70

In February 1960 Cecil Beer handed over the chairmanship of MK to Robert Dunstone (see Appendix). He in turn was backed up by two joint secretaries, K. Chetwood-Aiken and Stephen Fuller, the latter a founder-member and the editor of the *Padstow Echo*. The movement that they inherited had been forged during a period of growing concern over both the ethnic and economic future of Cornwall. Its creation seemed to represent a radical departure from the former antiquarian concerns of the Celtic Revival and was an opportunity to bring Cornwall in line with developments taking place in Scotland and Wales. But the movement that developed during the formative period of the 1950s could not escape from the cultural legacy of the past. Helena Charles had found it increasingly difficult during her period as leader to unite the group around a political agenda. Beer only succeeded in keeping MK together by reverting to a simpler form of nationalism that was acceptable to the wider Cornish movement. By 1960 MK was still a relatively small force but the crucial point was that it had survived. A framework was now in place for MK to move forward into the 1960s. With the Liberals now articulating an anti-metropolitan agenda, some saw an opportunity to advance the cause of Cornish nationalism in the electoral arena. However, the Liberals' growing support in the 1964 General Election also threatened to occupy any potential ground for a separate nationalist party, especially given MK's extremely cautious approach.

In the 1960s Cornwall also began to undergo a social revolution. The long decades of relative torpor since the disastrous decline of deep mining in the late 19th century and early 20th century, years interrupted only by the occasional economic 'false dawn', as in the Edwardian period and the later 1940s, were coming to an end. On all fronts things began to change. Economically, a new wave of industrial estates heralded the coming of light industry. Many of the firms attracted to these 'rural' industrial locations were from up-country, lured by regional grant aid, low wages and an available pool of female labour. The age of the branch plant economy had dawned. Demographically, the trickle of elderly retirees, mainly to coastal parishes, turned in the 1960s into a flood of working age migrants from the suburbs of the south east of England, lured by the prospect of an 'unspoilt' environment and encouraged by memories implanted during holiday visits. Their moves were facilitated by the savings accumulated during the boom years of the 1950s and by the knock-down house prices they found in Cornwall.

These developments were eventually to change Cornwall irrevocably. And in doing so they also, indirectly, catapulted MK from its rather cosy nostalgic cultural nationalism of the late 1950s into the more politicised, if not unambiguously political, nationalism of the 1970s. The early 1960s, therefore, were the calm before the storm, a period when MK trod water but also one in which, with hindsight, we can spot the harbingers of change massing on the horizon.

In the early days of Robert Dunstone's chairmanship, MK still operated at a fairly low level of activity. Despite the talk of forming branches in the late 1950s no permanent branch had in fact emerged. Instead, all members were free to attend the society's meetings, in 1961 held just once every six months. From March 1961 to October 1962 a fluctuating group of from 15 to 20 members attended these infrequent get-togethers, involving a core of ten plus another twenty or so who turned up on a less regular basis. The 30 names recorded in the minutes of these meetings actually made up a high proportion of the total paid up membership, which in March 1962 stood at just 70.[1] Members were painfully aware of the small size of the organisation. This was one reason why a move in March 1961 to publish a list of members was rejected as it 'would automatically reveal our numerical weakness' and undermine MK's credibility when petitioning the 'powers that be'. Moreover, Cecil Beer reported at this meeting that there had been 'an occasion during his chairmanship when he had been quietly asked to give up MK to try to re-form Tyr ha Tavas instead'.[2] Given that, by the late 1950s, MK's cultural nationalism was very close to the position of Tyr ha Tavas, it is difficult to see what would have been gained by such a move. Members were aware that there was a vicious circle at work. Because of its relative inactivity MK was not attracting many new members (around 12–16 a year at this point) and, equally important, current members were not renewing their subscriptions. As George Pawley White observed, this was not surprising as the impression was that 'MK had become defunct'.[3]

MK's numerical weakness was no doubt one of the factors which produced a defensive sensitivity towards outside bodies. This was clearly seen in attitudes towards the burgeoning mass media. Despite the growing role of television in society, MK was reluctant to embrace this new technology. Cecil Beer urged caution in dealing with the new ITV station in 1961 'on account of the risk of our being ridiculed'.[4] Similarly, in May 1962 the activities of a TV documentary producer, who contacted several MK members, caused some consternation. It was agreed that MK could provide 'little material for him and certainly nothing sensational', but that MK members might give information to journalists 'if this was restrained'.[5] Perhaps unsurprisingly, later in the same year a proposal to establish a press secretary was not approved. Suspicion of the outside world extended even to other 'Celtic' organisations. In 1961 the news of the intended formation of the Celtic League was greeted with some hesitation: 'we do not know enough about the League and the people who formed it'.[6] A year on, satisfied by its credentials, MK had not only joined the League but had proposed the first Cornish National Secretary, Roy Green. Indeed, in its early days the Celtic League seems to have been a part of MK rather than a separate organisation.

Inevitably, a large chunk of the business at these MK meetings was taken up with discussion of calendars, Christmas cards, serviettes, Cornish language classes and proposals for things like the Cornish kilt (which members agreed should be black in colour and not tartan). Nevertheless, change was in the air. MK did discuss economic issues such as the Cornish fishing industry or the proposed re-opening of a tin mine at Zennor and its environmental implications. It had also provided a submission for the Pilkington Committee on Broadcasting in 1960. This Committee did not publish MK's submission in its report but, in an interesting echo of government responses to Cornish lobbying in the 21st century, MK was told that 'non-publication did not mean our submission had been ignored'.[7] But it was difficult to reach any other conclusion.

Signs of change

Moreover, in 1962 there was a detectable quickening of the MK pulse. In that year the meetings became quarterly, there was again talk of holding district meetings where 'free and frank discussion' could take place and the admission of non-Cornish supporters to the Kerens Vebyon Kernow status of associate membership opened up a role in MK for sympathetic newcomers. But, more crucially, MK took an important step in late 1962 when it became more publicly involved in the issue of transport policy following the announcement of the proposed closure of railway branch lines. At first, in a familiar example of the way MK reacted to events, the organisation merely wrote letters of protest. But, this time, it was not content to stop there. Roy Green, a geography lecturer at Cornwall Technical College, had joined MK in March 1962, and together with Chetwood-

Aiken and John Finlayson (another new member) produced a report on the railway closures and formed a transport sub-committee of MK. This then called a public meeting at Truro, attracting 30 people.[8] As a result the Cornwall Transport Committee was formed, demanding what would now be called an integrated transport system for Cornwall. More important for the development of MK, the organisation had made an important and symbolic step towards a more public campaigning role. This was an indication of both a slowly growing confidence and a more visible presence of MK in Cornish life as the 1960s proceeded.

MK's campaigning style under Robert Dunstone throughout the early 1960s continued to be patient, persistent, and polite lobbying. Industrial development and a Cornish university joined better transport as issues for promotion. Such pressure group politics accompanied exceptionally close insider links with the Cornwall County Council chairman Alderman Kimberley Foster, links reflected in regular supportive communication between Dunstone and Foster. In 1966, for example, MK united with the Council to oppose the amalgamation of the Cornish and Devonian police forces. This was an early example of what later became termed by party activists 'Devonwall'. Elements in the new Labour Government of 1964, transfixed by what they saw as a 'technological revolution', were keen to re-organise government along more 'efficient' lines. However, in the drive for efficiency there was little place for nostalgic senses of place or local accountability. The Cornwall Police Force was deemed too small to be efficient so it was merged with the Devon force. As a result jobs in Cornwall filtered across the Tamar to the brand new police headquarters at Exeter. This began a process whereby managerial and professional jobs were steadily leached out of Cornwall, the inevitable result of centralising services on the cities of Plymouth, Exeter or Bristol. Interestingly, as MK pointed out, 'Devonwall' never seemed to result in headquarters being established in Cornwall. Supplementing campaigns for economic regeneration and institutional integrity was the ongoing more culturally based demand for a Cornish stamp. That at least resulted in the minister responsible, a certain Anthony Wedgwood Benn, giving Cornwall de-facto regional status when describing MK's demand as one for a 'regional postage stamp'.[9]

At the same time there were signs that MK members were more willing to come 'out of the closet'. The cloak of quasi-secrecy that had been adopted during the first decade of the movement was discarded in favour of a more public profile. The Falmouth branch even published a list of their officers in the *Falmouth Packet*. According to the branch secretary this was done 'to prove to the readers in the Packet that those people in Mebyon Kernow in the area were not "queer"'.[10] MK also began to receive some wider publicity. Robert Dunstone had already appeared on local BBC television in April 1964 and was interviewed in the William Hickey column of the *Daily Express* in August of the same year. Meanwhile, in 1965 the *Daily Telegraph* covered MK in a survey of 'fringe groups'.[11] While it reported that membership was around 700 and concluded that MK was no longer an 'intellectual fringe', the fact that this report was immediately followed by one on the Flat Earth Society did not do a great deal to enhance the status of the movement.

Nevertheless, the presence of branches, as at Falmouth, indicates that, by 1964, MK could finally sustain the branch structure that had been mooted at several earlier points. In January 1964 this was formalised and by early 1965 five branches were operating – Truro-Newquay, Falmouth-Penryn, Padstow, Penzance – and Nigeria! A branch structure increased the local presence of MK and indirectly led to the possibility of local electioneering, although in March 1962 a discussion on whether MK members should stand in local elections had resulted in the suggestion they put up instead as Independents. Robert Dunstone in particular dwelt on the difficulties posed by MK's lack of money.[12]

But it was two external developments that were to dramatically accelerate the growth of MK. In 1964 the new Greater London Council was set up. This authority soon began to seek ways to solve its planning difficulties and this search was destined indirectly to lead to a major increase in MK membership. Simultaneously, in the mid-1960s Celtic nationalism hit the headlines in a big way. In Wales Plaid Cymru had begun to win respectable votes as early as the 1955 General Election and in 1959 contested more than half the seats. But, as this had not led to the winning of parliamentary seats, it tended to be ignored by the Westminster-fixated political press correspondents. In 1966 it could be ignored no longer. Gwynfor Evans won Carmarthen on a record anti-government swing in July. In November of the following year Winnie Ewing showed that the nationalist surge was not confined to Wales by coming from nowhere to win the seat of Hamilton for the SNP. Suddenly Welsh and Scots nationalism were news. As they moved into the media spotlight there were straws in the wind that suggested that the success of Welsh and Scottish nationalist parties could have an echo in Cornwall. This was the context for a period of growth that marked the beginnings of MK's transformation from pressure group to political party.

Overspill

MK was soon to be taken more seriously, even by the London press. Growing publicity and new activity at branch level had already triggered off a gradual rise in membership. During 1967 it was asserted that membership rose three-fold and by early 1968 MK officers were confidently claiming 1,000 members.[13] In turn, rising support and the growth in the number of active branches to eleven by the end of 1967 generated more media coverage. The *Manchester Guardian* in December 1967 gave MK long and, by both earlier and later standards, very serious coverage. Detailing the 'growing support in the movement towards self-government for Cornwall' it concluded that 'there are some signs that Mebyon Kernow could become an organisation to be reckoned with'.[14] MK was beginning to be seen as a serious political organisation and this change in status resulted in a more populist stance and a new, much more public, profile for MK.

At the end of 1965, rumours of plans to build new towns of 50 to 60,000 people in order to accommodate the overspill of population from an overcrowded Greater London began to surface in Cornwall. MK was quick to contact Cornish local authorities urging their opposition to any such developments. Although it was soon decided that Cornwall was an unsuitable location for a whole new town, discussions in 1966 centred on more modest Town Development Schemes. Through these, towns outside London would enter agreements to house overspill population in return for industrial investment from Greater London. For some local planners the carrot was the guaranteed investment that would, they trusted, stimulate the local labour market and reverse the chronic problems of depopulation and low wages that Cornwall had known since the 1860s.

This carrot was enough to tempt many local councillors, as always desperate for some clearly visible symbol of regeneration. But it was met with derision by Mebyon Kernow. The movement was quick to reject the over-optimistic jobs creation forecast that came with the schemes. Members were appalled both by the GLC's use of Cornwall to solve its own planning problems and by the lack of confidence shown by local councillors in their own communities' abilities to solve endemic problems. In consequence MK vigorously opposed overspill from the beginning. In a pamphlet of 1967, MK asked 'are we second class citizens in our own land' and battled to make the issue one of Cornwall versus overspill.[15] While they viewed the economic arguments for overspill as fundamentally flawed, for most MK activists the threat to cultural identity was uppermost. As Donald Rawe wrote, overspill was seen as the 'worst threat to our independent self-respecting Cornishness since the forced introduction of the English prayer book in 1545' [*sic*]. He went on to compare it with the seventeenth century plantation of Ireland.[16] The English Prayer Book had led to a rising in 1549 that resulted in thousands of Cornish casualties and had helped deal a death blow to the sustainability of the Cornish language culture of the west of Cornwall. The results of the plantation in Ireland had borne and were still to bear disastrous fruit. These were thus strong words indeed, and underlined the sense of dismay felt by many Cornish activists at the impending population transfer.

Appeals to Cornwall's historic sense of identity did not, however, find much fertile ground amongst councillors numbed by a century of economic and cultural paralysis and lacking both a sense of confidence and a knowledge of Cornish history. Bodmin Town Council was the most eager to grasp the overspill offer. By April 1967 it had accepted it in principle and in January 1968 signed the first agreement for an overspill estate of 500 homes. MK responded by gathering a petition of 1,800 names in the spring and summer of 1968 in the town requesting a referendum. But the Town Council firmly set its face against this and, at the annual mayor-choosing ceremony in 1968, prominent councillors fell over themselves in their rush to attack MK. Their 'propaganda has failed miserably', claimed one prominent overspill supporter. The new mayor hoped that a 'vociferous minority' would not 'harm the future of our young people' while the old mayor thought 'nothing but good will come of (overspill)'.[17] Over a generation later a comparison of Bodmin with non-overspill towns would indicate that these hopes were sadly unfounded. Bodmin is no more obviously dynamic than any other town. Indeed, levels of social deprivation in the town remain stubbornly higher than in most parts of mid and east Cornwall.[18] Furthermore, in 2001, the two Bodmin County Council wards experienced the lowest voting turnout in Cornwall in that year's General Election, another indicator of a general alienation and a lack of involvement in the political process. In contrast, an early interest in overspill at Launceston soon evaporated and Liskeard Town Council had by the autumn of 1968 also rejected it. The main battleground, however, lay to the west, at Camborne-Redruth.

Here, in Cornwall's old but decaying industrial heartland, early interest in the promise of overspill led to discussions with the GLC in 1966, with all but two or three councillors in favour.[19] Although opposition rose to around a third of the total 30 councillors by 1967, it was decided to press ahead with a feasibility scheme for 1,000 overspill homes.[20] Paradoxically, this protracted and secretive process allowed MK to expand rapidly in the Camborne-Redruth area. Demands for a referendum, an opinion poll at Camborne and a series of letters to the local press kept the issue in the news. In April 1967 this bore fruit in the election of MK's first official councillor on Cornwall County Council. At St. Day and Lanner, Colin Murley (see Appendix) narrowly defeated Ken Stead, an urban district councillor and well known local Liberal who had consistently supported overspill talks, by a three vote margin. This victory was even more remarkable in that Colin Murley did not actually live in the ward but ten miles to the west, at Hayle. His election leaflets clearly called for 'independence in domestic affairs' and stated that 'no-one will take Cornwall seriously until she asserts her national status'.

Entering the electoral waters

St. Day and Lanner – MK's own Carmarthen or Hamilton – was the most spectacular outcome of a series of electoral interventions that had begun two years earlier in 1965. After Helena Charles' electioneering in the early 1950s, MK had not officially contested any local elections, although members had been returned as Independents. That changed in the mid-1960s and the years from 1965 to 1970 can be viewed as the first of three waves of electoral activity, the second occurring in 1977–81 and the third from 1993 onwards. But this was not the result of a considered strategy. Mebyon Kernow stumbled into standing official candidates in local elections almost by default. In 1965 the very active branch at Padstow decided to stand two candidates in the UDC elections. This was a place where close branch links with the Fishermen's Association combined with concern over the growing effects of tourism to make MK's message attractive and the two candidates, Frank Sluman and Len Prior, were duly returned, coming top and third in the poll. Simultaneously at Penryn, Eddie Murray, already a councillor, asked the local branch if he could stand as an official candidate. He did and was elected unopposed. These first three councillors were a milestone. MK had re-entered the electoral arena and, for Robert Dunstone at least, the success showed 'that the Cornish people are emerging from the somnolence of the past'.[21]

Nevertheless, this was a tentative and hesitant testing of the electoral temperature. Even at Padstow and Penryn official candidates did not necessarily mean that MK was 'political'. Eddie Murray stated in his election leaflet that 'As a Cornishman I feel that as a member of a non-political Cornish organisation I can best serve all of the community'. At Padstow in 1966 when three candidates stood, this time unsuccessfully, they clearly stated that MK was 'not a political party. It represents no sectional interests at all'.[22] Standing as official MK candidate was, if anything at this time, a reaffirmation of independence in local council chambers and a rejection of party politics. In addition to the three at Padstow, Michael Grigg stood for the Trevone ward of the Padstow UDC in 1966 and was elected unopposed. Ed Doney, a sitting councillor, then became a member and branch organiser Donald Rawe was co-opted, thus giving MK five seats on the council. In the same year, an MK candidate also stood in the Smithick ward of Falmouth, winning 47 per cent of the votes in a straight fight with Labour. There were also five candidates in 1967, and this time all stood in the overspill hotspot of Camborne-Redruth.

Two councillors, Clive Budden and George Harris, were elected unopposed at Illogan. Meanwhile, in Camborne, Bertha Hooper managed a solid result, beating three of the four Labour candidates to come fifth in a four-seat ward. At St. Day however, Morley Kinver could not replicate Colin Murley's earlier County Council victory, losing to the sitting Independent councillor.

MK election activity in this first wave peaked in the following year – 1968. Robert Heller fought a by-election to win a seat on Penwith Rural District Council at Hayle and then nine candidates stood across Cornwall in the main May elections, in Camborne-Redruth, Falmouth, Liskeard and Truro, while members also stood as Independents at Padstow, St. Austell and Bodmin. Other town and parish candidates and councillors had also joined MK in the upsurge of 1966–68 but preferred to remain more anonymous at the ballot box. By June of 1969, for example, Hayle branch was claiming six rural district councillors and two parish councillors as members, although only two had officially stood as MK candidates.[23] Another Independent was Perranporth county councillor Paul Thomas, who was also a member of the Conservative Party. Rumour later had it that he had been deputed by his party to join MK to see what it was up to. What the local Tories could not predict was that Paul was to 'go native', lending tacit support to MK Euro-candidates in the 1980s and developing a keen interest in Cornish history.

In 1968, despite the conclusion of the *West Briton* that 'the electorate had flatly rejected the Cornish nationalist anti-overspill platform',[24] MK candidates achieved very respectable votes and 23-year old Roger Holmes (see Appendix) was elected at Liskeard. Moreover, the *West Briton* failed to point out that an anti-overspill Labour candidate had topped the poll at Camborne while two other vociferously anti-overspill but not official MK candidates were elected and re-elected at Illogan North and Redruth. No doubt partly alarmed by the support MK and its sympathisers were receiving, a special meeting of Camborne-Redruth Urban District Council called to discuss the feasibility report on the Town Development Scheme in October 1968 finally rejected it[25] – a decision hailed by MK as a 'great victory'.

What Cornishmen can do

For long term MK activists the opposition to overspill was a logical and principled part of MK's opposition to 'those who would oppose our Cornish heritage and our Cornish way of life', as Robert Dunstone put it at the 1967 AGM. In this light the overspill campaign could be read as part of a 'wave of Celtic protest and progress'.[26] More broadly, for those of a romantic bent within the movement, here was the Cornish equivalent of those student revolts that had scorched across the universities of Europe and North America, or the May 'revolution' in France in 1968 or the upsurge of language militancy in both Wales and Brittany. Indeed, in those years some were attracted to the Cornish struggle precisely because it resonated with what were seen as wider campaigns of liberation.

Yet it also had its darker side. The *Manchester Guardian* had gone so far as to claim the growth of MK was 'attributed largely to fear'.[27] It was true that a number of those joining MK did not see much further than hostility to large-scale immigration from London. Indeed, opponents were quick to describe MK's opposition as 'racialist'. Such attacks had two effects. First, they forced MK's leadership to clarify the movement's position. Thus Len Truran, Camborne-Redruth branch organiser, differentiated overspill from voluntary 'settlers', saying that 'we in MK seek to serve *all* Cornishmen – whether they be by birth or adoption – without fear or favour'.[28] MK was thus slowly beginning to edge towards a more civic nationalist position.

Secondly, MK produced its own alternative to overspill. This came in the form of a pamphlet *What Cornishmen Can Do*, published in September 1968. This was the most comprehensive manifesto for Cornwall produced to date. Its proposals included some long standing MK grievances but also anticipated much of what has since become mainstream thinking. In *What Cornishmen Can Do* MK called for 'real' development based on Cornwall's natural resources, together with secondary industries that utilised those resources and took advantage of the 'technical genius' of the Cornish people. Other proposals included more emphasis on food processing, support for small farmers, the creation of a University of Cornwall, quality tourism with greater overseas marketing and the expansion of renewable energy through the construction of tidal barrages. Apart from the gender-bias of the title the report was far ahead of its times. It received sympathetic and factual coverage in the local press, although being trivialised by Westward TV, a harbinger of the Plymouth television coverage of MK that was later to become the norm. The economic proposals in this pamphlet became the resources for a harder edged, more conflictual campaigning style that became noticeable after 1968. MK press releases were now more likely to focus on the unfavourable comparison between Cornwall and the south east of England and even began to use the language of 'colonization'.

Into Parliament?

This new stance coincided with the election of a new chairman, as Len Truran (see Appendix) took over from Robert Dunstone in 1968. Before this change at the top, MK's position on fighting elections had moved up a gear. In the mid-1960s there was growing discussion by the MK leadership about the possibility of fighting parliamentary elections. A well attended AGM in 1967 at the height of the overspill agitation had, 'after much discussion', decided to press ahead with preparations to fight the next General Election, instructing the National Executive Committee to prepare a list of prospective candidates. But as soon as the decision was taken it began to run into problems. Many of those who had pitched up with MK in the mid-1960s had retained their membership of the London based political parties. The most prominent of these were of course the two Liberal MPs, Peter Bessell and John Pardoe, together with David Mudd who had joined in July 1966 and, one year later, had been selected as Conservative Prospective Parliamentary Candidate for Falmouth-Camborne.

Such dual membership was common in the mid-1960s. MK was at that time viewed by most people who joined as primarily a pro-Cornish pressure group. In particular, membership of MK and the Liberal Party was not seen as incompatible. Indeed, during the late 1960s MK continued to receive offers of collaboration from the Liberals. In October 1968 the Liberal Party agent in North Cornwall proposed an electoral pact, saying that Liberals had been campaigning for the policies in *What Cornishmen Can Do* for years and shared common cause with MK. Liberals still made occasional public calls for self-government for Cornwall and the Liberal Constituency Associations in 1968 were reported to be 'investigating the political and economic implications of independence' and considering a bill demanding independence for Cornwall.[29] MK's role as a pressure group during the 1950s and 1960s had seemingly brought it considerable recognition and forced the Liberals into some clarification of their public stance in favour of devolution. It was thus by no means clear in the 1965–69 period that MK's inevitable trajectory was to become a political party. Nevertheless, the MK leadership, perhaps emboldened by the relatively poor Liberal performance in West Cornwall in the 1966 General Election, stuck to the decision made by the 1967 AGM to fight Parliamentary elections and rejected Liberal overtures. The die was seemingly cast. Although dual membership was still possible this decision was bound to cause a crisis of loyalty for such members.

Predictably enough, support began to leak away almost as soon as the 1967 decision was made. The fallout was immediately felt as the two elected MK councillors in Illogan, both Liberals, publicly disassociated themselves from the decision in December of 1967. Confusion continued well into 1969. In September 1968 the Launceston branch was seeking clarification in *Cornish Nation* on MK's position on 'party politics'. As late as May 1969 Redruth members at their branch meeting were still unsure whether there was to be a parliamentary candidate or not. This confusion is odd, as the decision had in fact already been made to stand a candidate in the Falmouth-Camborne constituency.[30] It may have been a symptom of a lack of internal communication. Or, more likely, it betrayed a certain ambivalence, even opposition, in respect of the decision to stand Parliamentary candidates in the first place.

The overspill-induced boost in membership had created the impression of a widespread popular support which seemed to promise success in the electoral arena. Nevertheless, it became clear that many of those who had joined did not share the nationalist assumptions of the older leadership core of MK. A large number were in MK primarily for local motives. As early as 1966 one prominent founder member was bemoaning the way many at the AGM had no interest in the other Celtic countries, Cornwall's Celtic heritage or international co-operation. Instead, their concerns were 'narrow and parochial' and there was a danger that MK would be 'turned into a glorified Cornish Ratepayers Association which merely grumbles about present grievances and loses sight of the long-term aims'.[31] Misunderstandings about exactly what MK stood for were evident in 1969 during a dispute at Falmouth over the right of pleasure boats to fly the St. Piran's flag. The chairman of the Falmouth branch was quoted as saying 'we want our identity, that's all. We want a united Great Britain, not home rule for Cornwall'.[32] At this time official MK policy remained domestic self-government for Cornwall. Competing assumptions about what MK stood for tended be played down within the organisation, yet they did not bode well for an election intervention during which the pressures of campaigning and the need to clarify policy could strain what was in effect a wide-ranging coalition of interests.

Despite these problems, Richard Jenkin duly went forward on a platform of 'internal self-government' and the proposals outlined in the *What Cornishmen Can Do* pamphlet. He won 960 votes, or 2.0 per cent of the total. Immediately post-election, a brave face was put on the results. According to Len Truran intervention achieved its objective: 'We had an enormous effect on the election in Cornwall. We suddenly had 15 candidates speaking like Cornishmen'.[33] In reality however, organisational problems had been evident even before the election, accompanying the sense of anti-climax that set in once the overspill row subsided. In the local elections of 1969 only four official MK candidates had stood, although Tim Richards won a seat at Penzance and Gerry Garnish was elected unopposed at Hayle. In 1970, two stood for Truro Town Council and one at Falmouth, while two members were elected in Padstow but not as official candidates. Indeed, becoming more overtly 'political' in fighting the parliamentary seat may have resulted in branches and members in areas like Padstow stepping back from presenting themselves as official MK candidates. This partly explains the lack of explicit electoral activity in the 1970–74 period, when MK members preferred to campaign as Independents and declined to use the MK label.

This decrease in electoral activity occurred within the context of MK's first split. In July of 1969 several active members, dissatisfied with the continuing possibility of dual membership of MK and other parties and by the snail-like speed with which MK was being transformed into a political nationalist party, had formed the Cornish National Party at Redruth. The dissidents felt that, as MK comprised a broad and varied membership, holding 'every imaginable view from extreme nationalism to the exact opposite … it has proved impossible to agree on a consistent, workable policy of nationalism'.[34] The principal concern of the new CNP was the refusal by MK to proclaim itself a political party and, interestingly, two of its leading lights had been MK elected councillors: Roger Holmes, who became leader of the new party, and Colin Murley. The basic aims of the CNP were, however, very similar to those of MK, being to 'seek self-government for Cornwall, and to secure the rightful recognition of Cornwall as a Celtic Nation and not as an English county'. In the first instance many CNP members felt that continued membership of both MK and the CNP was possible, on the grounds that the former was a cross-party pressure group and the latter a nationalist political party. But the MK NEC disagreed and narrowly expelled the CNP members, by a margin of two votes with two abstentions.[35]

This was the first of three major splits in the organisation at roughly five year intervals – 1969, 1975, 1980 – two of which led to alternative Cornish nationalist parties. Yet, in the immediate aftermath of the split, the three CNP candidates in the 1970 county council elections (Roger Holmes at Liskeard, Len Trelease at St. Day and Colin Murley at Penzance) were no more successful than the two from MK (Tim Richards at Penzance and Dr A. Ash at Bude-Stratton). Furthermore, as the MK leadership had decided to continue to pursue its parliamentary election strategy, in spite of the ambiguity of much of its membership towards the idea, there was little space for another organisation with very similar aims. The CNP gradually faded out of view, many of its members drifting back to MK by the mid-1970s.

As Richard Jenkin later argued, the formation of the CNP just a few months before the 1970 General Election had hardly helped the cause, acting, in his words, as a 'distraction' which 'prevented the campaign from being as effective as it might have been'.[36] In hindsight the decision to fight Falmouth-Camborne, while making sense in that it included MK's largest branches, was a strange one. For Richard Jenkin was up against two candidates who had themselves been, and perhaps still were, MK

(1) Louis C. Duncoombe-Jewell at 1904 Celtic Congress in Caernarfon

(2) Henry Jenner at 1928 Gorseth at Boscawen-Un

(3) Henry Jenner addressing 1932 Celtic Congress at Menabilly

(4) The chough logo of the Tyr ha Tavas organisation

(5) Participants at the Truro Celtic Congress held in 1950

(6) Leading members of MK outside the building formerly known as Oates
Temperance Hotel in Redruth to mark MK's 50th anniversary

(7) Helena Charles, MK Chair
1951-1956

(8) Major Cecil Beer, MK Chairman
1956-1960

(9) E. G. Retallack Hooper being installed as Grand Bard in 1959

(10) Robert Dunstone,
MK Chairman 1960-1968

(11) MK's first treasurer
George Pawley White pictured
in 1964

DHE COF A
MYCHAL JOSEP
AN COF
HA
THOMAS FLAMANK
HEMBRYNKYSY AN LU KERNEWEK
A CESKERDHAS BYS DHE LOUNDRES
HA CODHEVEL ENA DYALANS
METHEVEN 1497
"Y A'S TEVYTH HANOW A
BES VYNYTHA HA BRY A DHUR
HEP MERWEL"
DREHEVYS GANS MEBYON KERNOW.
1966

IN MEMORY OF
MICHAEL JOSEPH
THE SMITH
AND
THOMAS FLAMANK
LEADERS OF THE CORNISH HOST
WHO MARCHED TO LONDON
AND SUFFERED VENGEANCE THERE
JUNE 1497
"THEY SHALL HAVE A NAME
PERPETUAL AND A FAME PERMANENT
AND IMMORTAL"
ERECTED BY MEBYON KERNOW.
1966

(12) Memorial to 1497 rebels erected by MK in 1966

(13) Colin Murley and helpers at 1967 St Day and
Lanner by-election

(14) Home-made sign in St Day hedge for council by-election

(15) Popular 1960s poster calling for Cornish self-government

(16) Peter Bessell, Liberal MP for
Bodmin 1964-1970 and
MK member

(17) John Pardoe, Liberal MP for North Cornwall
1966-1979 and MK member

(18) Len Truran, Richard Jenkin and Geoffrey Proctor handing in
nominations for 1970 General Election

(19) On the campaign trail in the Falmouth-Camborne constituency

MEBYON KERNOW

⊕

A VOTE FOR

JENKIN

is a VOTE for

CORNWALL

Published by L. H. Truran, Trewirgie Hill, Redruth.   Printed by J. & M. Roberts, Trewirgie Road, Redruth.

(20) 1970 General Election poster for Richard Jenkin

(21) Cartoon from Cornish Nation magazine (December 1970)

(22) Cartoon from Cornish Nation magazine (June 1971)

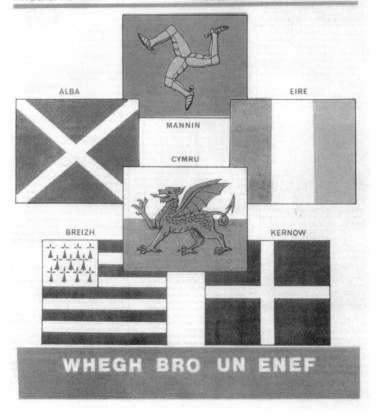

(23) The controversial 1974 Cornish Nation which included feature on Michael Gaughan

(24) Dr James Whetter, editor of Cornish Nation 1970-1975 and
CNP leader from 1975

(25) An Gof Commemoration at St Keverne in June 1975

(26) Redruth rally against unemployment in October 1977

(27) Penzance rally for Cornish fishing in November 1978

(28) Roger Holmes speaking at Penzance fishing rally

(29) St. Ives candidate Colin Murley in 1978

(30) Len Truran, MK Chairman 1968–73,
on the campaign trail

(31) Richard Jenkin,
MK Chairman 1973–83,
as MK Euro-candidate in 1979

(32) Pedyr Prior, MK Chairman 1985-1986, (standing third from left) and
St Just councillor Malcolm Williams (seated) with St Ives
branch members in 1978

(33) Advert in Redruth-Camborne Packet for 1979 local elections

(34) MK picket at Redruth Job Centre in 1980

(35) Mebyon Kernow activists occupying drilling rig at Luxulyan

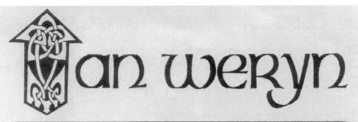

an weryn

No 13. Summer 1980   15p

inside —

NUCLEAR HORRORS

UNEMPLOYMENT
HOUSING ASSOCIATIONS
ECO MOVEMENT — FACTS AND
                    FIGURES
AND MUCH MORE!

LATE FLASH!

M.K. extremists

in Nude bathing

scare

cornwall's radical magazine

(36) An Weryn magazine (Summer 1980)

gwyn ha du

NUMBER 6
SUMMER 1982

INSIDE:-

JULYAN DREW INTERVIEW;
THE 'FALKLANDS WAR';
CRUISE MISSILE HITS BREAD VAN;
+ NEWS + COMMENT.......

ALL FOR ONLY...... **25P**

yn mes a dhethel, an desmyk - out of argument, the answer

«ONEN HAG OLL»

IS DIVISIVE !!

Support for the Cornish Language, traditionally, has always come from the Cornish Gorseth. It would seem that is no longer the case. The Gorseth Council recently voted against a proposal, putbefore it, to call upon the Cornwall Council to change its motto of "One and All" to read the Cornish "Onen Hag Oll". The proposal was rejected upon the grounds that it would not be understood..........

Continued page five.....

M.K. WIN

IN PENWITH....

TWENTY TWO YEAR OLD COLIN LAWRY SECRETARY OF MOUNTS BAY MEBYON KERNOW WAS ELECTED TO PENWITH DISTRICT COUNCIL IN THE MAY ELECTIONS. He beat Conservative Mrs Doreen Rabbite by over 130 votes becoming the first official MK member on Penwith Council. In nearby St.Just, MK Candidate, Malcolm Williams came second in a four way fight pushing the SDP / Liberal Alliance candidate into last place.

The 1982 Penwith Campaign was arguably one of the best organised the party has yet fought with over 100 workers in the field. Help came from as far as Liskeard and Falmouth to aid the two MK Candidates.

M.K. District Councillor Colin Lawry

...AND IN FALMOUTH

the party has another Councillor in Mary Wincott. Mary was elected unopposed to Falmouth Town Council after the death of the sitting Labour member.
All this and more pages two and three.

Penzance Central Results:

Voting: C. Lawry, 566; Mrs D. Rabbitte, 433; Percentage poll 34.9

(37) Gwyn ha Du magazine (Summer 1982)

(38) Julyan Drew, MK
Chairman 1983-1985

(39) Loveday Carlyon, MK Chair
1986-1989

(40) Poster widely circulated by the Cornwall Concern Group in 1987

Peninsula

No. 69 NOVEMBER 1988

VOICe

News from Penzance, St Ives, St Just & the Penwith area

60p

MEBYON
KERNOW:
Dead
or
Alive?

(41) 1988 Peninsula Voice magazine featuring Colin Lawry

(42) Colin Lawry, leading MK
councillor from 1982-2002

(43) Loveday Jenkin,
MK Chair 1990-1997

(44) Anti-poll tax graffiti in Liskeard in 1990

(45) Tom Tremewan, winner of 1994 Carrick District Council by-election

(46) 1997 General Election candidates; John Bolitho, Ruth Lewarne,
Paul Dunbar and Davyth Hicks

(47) Start of Kerkerdh Kernow 500 march in St Keverne, June 1997

(48) Demonstration at gates of South Crofty tin mine

(49) Dick Cole, MK Leader 1997 - present, addressing Cornish Solidarity demonstration at Tamar Bridge in 1998

(50) MK candidates for 1999 district council elections

(51) Cornish graffiti on regional development agency signs

(52) Hilda Wasley launches
declaration campaign
in March 2000

(53) Bert Biscoe, Stephen Horscroft, Andrew George MP, Nick Serpell and Dick Cole at launch of Cornish Constitutional Convention

(54) Dean Shipton signs 20,000th declaration in December 2000

(55) 2001 General Election candidates; Conan Jenkin,
Hilda Wasley and Ken George

(56) Phil Rendle, MK district councillor elected in 2002

Camborne-Redruth Urban District Council
St. Day, Carharrack and Lanner Ward
POLLING DAY:—WEDNESDAY, DECEMBER 30th, 1953

HIGHER NINNIS, ST. DAY.

Ladies and Gentlemen of St. Day, Carharrack and Lanner,

In asking you to elect me as your representative on the Camborne-Redruth Urban District Council, I am not making any promises that I cannot fulfil. I can only say that as I suffer myself from the lack of water supply and sanitation, I have every reason to do all in my power to remedy this state of affairs.

As I know only too well the misery that results from lack of housing, I shall do my best to see that houses are not only built, but fairly allocated. The other great evil and danger to family life, unemployment, is also of special concern to me, and I shall support any scheme that seems likely to reduce it.

Though I was taken away from Cornwall as a small child, it has always been my hope to return home and do my bit for the Cornish people. At present hundreds of young Cornish people leave Cornwall every year, because there are no jobs for them. Their place is taken by elderly people from up the country, who retire to a warm climate. Few of the best jobs are held by Cornish people. This is not just.

I believe that everyone has the right and duty to develop in his natural community, and that each community, including Cornwall, has a special contribution to make to the international community that we must build if mankind is to survive. I have just returned from the Continent where I was representing the Sons of Cornwall at a gathering of small communities.

Until the Government of Britain is decentralised, and local government made really responsible for local affairs, we shall continue to endure the present state of affairs, in which an anonymous clerk, in Bristol or London, can make decisions vitally affecting the rates in this Urban District. This devolution of power can only come about if voters in Cornwall, and elsewhere, accept their responsibilities as electors.

In conclusion, I would say that I not only have experience of the problems of local government, but leisure which will enable me to be of service to the ward.

Yours sincerely,
HELENA TREVELYAN E. CHARLES.

ON DECEMBER 30th, VOTE FOR
X **CHARLES** X
and a square deal for the Cornish

Printed and Published by P. R. Earle & Co., Station Hill, Redruth. Phone 199

(57) Helena Charles' election leaflet for Redruth-Camborne UDC, 1953

To the Electors of the Borough of Penryn

Ladies and Gentlemen,

Having served you faithfully and to the best of my ability since July 1963, my term of office is now expired and once again I place myself before you for your consideration.

I have always tried to act fairly and without bias for all members of the community and have on many occasions spoken my mind with your interests at heart.

I have been invited by the Penryn Pendennis Branch of Mebyon Kernow (Sons of Cornwall) to stand as a candidate in the Borough Election. My reasons for accepting are simple - to anyone who has the interests of PENRYN and CORNWALL at heart. As a Cornishman I feel that as a member of a non political Cornish organisation I can best serve all of the community.

I am most strongly opposed to any form of amalgamation of the Borough and pledge that I shall fight for the retention of our Borough status. I feel that Penryn can and always will manage her own affairs without outside interference. Why should we, steeped as we are in ancient history and tradition, become the industrial suburb of Falmouth?

Penryn has the factories, providing a vital link in the serious unemployment situation in the district. Due to the foresight of a far seeing and go-ahead council this is not just a dream on a drawing board.

A vote for a MEBYON KERNOW candidate is a VOTE FOR PENRYN. Please give me your vote to enable me to protect your interests.

Yours sincerely,

E. Murray

9 Saracen Crescent, Penryn, Cornwall.

VOTE FOR MURRAY
Your Cornish Candidate

Penryn Municipal Election, Thursday the 13th of May 1965

Published by Mr. E. A. G. Webber, 1 Commercial Rd., Penryn. Printed by W. Chapman

(58) Eddie Murray's election leaflet for Penryn UDC, 1965

MEBYON KERNOW

VOTE

| TRURAN | X |

LIB·LAB·TORY HAVE HAD THEIR DAY
VOTE MEBYON KERNOW THE CORNISHWAY
PARLIAMENTARY ELECTION 1979
THURSDAY MAY 3rd

PLEASE DISPLAY THIS IN YOUR WINDOW

Published by Neil Plummer, Blythe, New Road, Stythyans.
Printed by Penzance Printers, 48 Causewayhead, Penzance.

(59) Len Truran's 1979 General Election leaflet for Falmouth-Camborne

Election Communication

GENERAL ELECTION
TRURO & ST AUSTELL CONSTITUENCY
Thursday 7th June 2001

Conan
JENKIN

Mebyon Kernow

The Party for Cornwall

VOTE FOR CORNWALL

In this election, the people of Truro and St Austell have an important choice to make. You can either vote for one of the London parties, all absorbed in Westminster's political games. Or you can vote for Mebyon Kernow - the Party for Cornwall and put Cornwall on the map.

Only a vote for Mebyon Kernow – the Party for Cornwall will make the government sit up and take notice of Cornwall. **Support for Mebyon Kernow is a message that no London politician can ignore.**

PUBLISHED BY C JENKIN, 39 DANIELL RD, TRURO. PRINTED BY REDBORNE PRINTERS, REDRUTH.

(60) Conan Jenkin's 2001 General Election leaflet for Truro and St Austell

members. One was David Mudd, who went on to win the seat from Labour; the other was the Liberals' Jon Davey, a well-established local councillor who had led the opposition to overspill on Camborne-Redruth Urban District Council. In such circumstances the difference between MK and Tory/Liberal candidates was relatively subtle. Moreover, the marginal nature of the constituency militated against a large MK vote. For a short period Robert Flamank had been a candidate at St. Ives, before being forced to pull out because of illness. This was perhaps a pity in view of the less marginal character of that seat and the clearer water between MK and the local representatives of the London parties. Given the later results in 1979 we might speculate that MK's vote in the St. Ives constituency might have been somewhat higher, thus doing more to establish the organisation's visibility at the beginning of the 1970s.

The 1960s was a crucial decade, perhaps the crucial decade, in MK's history. In those years the organisation, by deciding to fight Parliamentary elections, took a decisive step towards establishing itself as a nationalist party on the lines of the SNP or Plaid Cymru. However, this decision appears in retrospect to have been made with little thought for the strategic consequences. The large proportion of MK members who preferred to view MK as a pressure group meant that MK's move into the electoral arena was ambiguous to say the least. There remained many members who, while supporting MK's demands, especially in the cultural field, preferred to work politically for the Liberal Party. Indeed, the resurgent Liberal Party posed a huge dilemma for MK as here was a more credible and already established home for anti-metropolitan sentiment and for the protest voter. Fighting Parliamentary elections in the absence of a strong local base and a membership wholly committed to electoral politics exposed MK's core support in 1970 as woefully weaker than that for the nationalist parties in Scotland and Wales. Nonetheless, the 960 votes for MK at Falmouth-Camborne in 1970 was a higher proportion than the 609 won by Plaid Cymru in its first election contest at Caernarfon in 1929. And yet by 1970 Plaid was coming a close second in the same constituency and threatening the sitting Labour MP. The question for the 1970s was whether MK's activists had the stamina for a similarly long haul.

Notes

1. Minutes of MK meetings, Mar 25 1961–Oct 27 1962, MK Collection.
2. Minutes of MK AGM, 25 March 1961, MK Collection.
3. Minutes of MK meeting, 30 September 1961, MK Collection.
4. Minutes of MK AGM, 25 March 1961, MK Collection.
5. Minutes of MK meeting, 26 May 1962, MK Collection.

6. Minutes of MK meeting, 30 September 1962, MK Collection.
7. Minutes of MK meeting, 26 May 1962, MK Collection.
8. Report of meeting to protest about rail closures 1962, MK Collection.
9. Letter from Anthony Wedgwood Benn to Peter Bessell, 10 February 1965, MK Collection.
10. Press cutting, *Falmouth Packet*, c. 1965, MK Collection.
11. Press cuttings, *Daily Express* and *Daily Telegraph*, 1964–65, MK Collection.
12. Minutes of MK AGM, 25 March 1961, MK Collection.
13. *Scotsman*, 10 February 1968.
14. *Guardian*, 5 December 1967.
15. MK (1967), *Cornwall v. Overspill*, Truro.
16. *Cornish Guardian*, 27 February 1967.
17. *Western Morning News*, 22 May 1968.
18. Sarah Payne (1996), *Poverty and Deprivation in West Cornwall in the 1990s*, Bristol.
19. Camborne-Redruth Urban District Council minutes, 31 October 1966.
20. Camborne-Redruth UDC minutes, 24 July 1967.
21. Press cutting, *Sunday Independent*, 1965, MK Collection.
22. *Cornish Guardian*, 28 April 1966.
23. List of MK Hayle branch officers, 27 June 1969, MK Collection.
24. *West Briton*, 16 May 1968.
25. Camborne-Redruth UDC minutes, 16 October 1968.
26. *West Briton*, 20 November 1967.
27. *Guardian*, 5 December 1967.
28. *West Briton*, 25 May 1967.
29. Press cutting, *West Briton*, 1968; MK Collection and see Garry Tregidga (2000), '"Bodmin Man": Peter Bessell and Cornish Politics in the 1950s and 1960s', *Cornish Studies, Eight*, pp. 161–181.
30. *Cornish Nation*, Vol. 1. 5 (January/February 1969). *Cornish Nation* was first published in duplicated form in 1967 by Len Truran. It was immediately relaunched as 'Cornwall's first truly national newspaper' later that same year under new editor Derek Tozer of Launceston (1968–69). The magazine appeared, somewhat sporadically up until 1982, under the editorships of James Whetter (1970–1975), Donald Rawe (1976–77), Julyan Holmes and Pedyr Prior (1978–1979), Julyan Holmes (1980–81) and Neil Plummer (1982). *Cornish Nation* was relaunched in 1993 and continues to the present day. In the absence of a party magazine in the mid 1980s, an attempt was made to launch a new journal called *Cornish Voice*, by an editorial team of Loveday Carlyon, Julyan Holmes and Pedyr Prior. It folded after only one edition.
31. Letter from R.G. Jenkin to Robert Dunstone, June 1966, MK Collection.
32. *Falmouth Packet*, 12 September 1969.
33. *Sunday Independent*, 21 June 1970.
34. Letter from Len Trelease and Roger Holmes to MK National Executive, July 1969, MK Collection.
35. Minutes of MK NEC, July 1969.
36. Richard Jenkin (1991), *40 Years of Mebyon Kernow*, Leedstown.

V

CHANGING DIRECTION: 1970–80

The 1970s were the years in which MK took a decisive step towards becoming an election-fighting political party, breaking out of the cultural pressure group role bequeathed to it by its founders. By the end of the decade the organisation had proved that it could fight election campaigns at all levels, from parish to European, and it had begun to compete credibly with the other political parties. While there were still moments of doubt and uncertainty to come, by 1979 MK was well on the road to becoming a political party. Nonetheless, this was by no means certain at the beginning of the decade. The 1970s began with a sense of anti-climax following on the depressing election result of 1970 and the split that occasioned the Cornish National Party. And things were to get worse before they began to get better.

In the early part of 1970 John Fleet formed MK's Cowethas Flamank research and lobbying group made up of Cornish exiles. Yet, even this enthusiastic and indefatigably-led band of supporters were forced to admit in 1971 that 'an unhappy malaise ... a general lack of confidence and of sense of purpose' had set in after the split of 1969 and the uncertainties that followed the General Election of 1970.[1] And yet there was hardly a lack of issues. In 1969 the Maud Report had proposed a restructuring of local government. The more radical proposals of this Commission were not accepted by the Labour Government but by March 1970 it was clear that local government reorganisation was going to lead to the transfer of St. Germans Rural District Council, together with Saltash and Torpoint boroughs, into a new Tamarside authority. MK furiously denounced this: 'any erosion of our traditional borders whether they be along the Tamar in the south or the Marsland to the north, would be bitterly resented by all true Cornishmen'.[2] In the event the unexpected Tory victory in the 1970 general election led to the shelving of the proposal and, despite a rearguard action by Plymouth City Council in 1971, the integrity of the Cornish boundary was assured.

At the same time, worried by the growth of Plaid Cymru and SNP, the

British Government had resorted to the time-honoured stalling device of a Royal Commission. The Crowther (later Kilbrandon) Commission set out to take evidence about devolution and in May 1971 representatives from MK, the CNP and the Celtic League united to give evidence to this Commission and to demand Cornish self-government. They were heard out for an hour, with 'polite disdain' according to one of the delegates, but at least placed on record the Cornish case in this major review of constitutional arrangements.[3] On a more mundane level, MK continued to lobby in these years in a reactive way against developments that affected Cornwall's integrity or its quality of life. These ranged from opposition to Concorde booms to objections to the South West Economic Planning Council's economic regions and to the imposition of Plymouth (PL) and Exeter (EX) postcodes. After 1971, signs of re-energised vigour on the part of the organisation slowly began to re-appear. Cowethas Flamank began to produce useful data on border blurring and constitutional options; Bert Boyd at Illogan suggested the formation of working groups of active members to supplement the branch structure and to rouse people from their apathy; and finally, *Cornish Nation*, which had first appeared in late 1967 but hit the buffers in late 1969, re-established a regular publication timetable under the editorship of James Whetter (see Appendix).

Migration and housing pressures

The context of the 1970s was notably less encouraging than the mid-1960s. In 1972 and 1973 it began to dawn on MK members that the victory against overspill had been a hollow one. Planned schemes of population migration may have been defeated but the voluntary movement of very large numbers of people into Cornwall was already quietly under way even as the debate raged over overspill. In the early 1970s this was fuelled by the short-lived 'Barber boom' as Ted Heath's government made a doomed 'dash for growth'. The resulting rise in house prices in the south east of England merely triggered a dash to Cornwall. Cornwall's population rose by 90,000, or 26 per cent, from 1961 to 1981, the fastest rate of growth since the 1830s and an increase that made the overspill plans of the 1960s look modest in comparison. While the overspill town of Bodmin saw a population growth of 96 per cent in these years, non-overspill towns like Saltash (75 per cent growth), Helston (60 per cent) and Liskeard (41 per cent) were not far behind. Counter-urbanisation was proceeding with a vengeance and Cornwall's population now began to rise faster than virtually anywhere else in the UK. Increased wealth in the overheating south east of England, a car-borne, more mobile population, the growth in second home ownership all meant that places like Cornwall were set to provide a small release valve for the more global pressures produced by post-war British economic growth. As both central and local government backed this process of 'counter-ur-banisation' MK looked to be in for a David and Goliath struggle.

With counter-urbanisation came rapid social change, a process per-haps most noticeable in the coastal areas. By the summer of 1972 MK's Camborne branch was complaining of too many houses sold to 'foreign-ers', worrying about 'winter ghost towns' and pointing out that St. Agnes was 'almost taken over by up-country people'. In September, a reported plan by the GLC to build an estate at Illogan for retired couples from London was condemned as 'overspill going through the back door'.[4] Such plans appeared even more of an insult when price inflation was driving first time buyers out of the market and local government was pruning back its council housing plans in the face of government cuts in spending. MK press releases in 1973 railed against the frenzy of land and property speculation, spoke of 'the desperate housing and economic situation developing in Cornwall' and demanded regulation of a tourist industry that was seen as helping to fuel these social and demographic changes. *Cornish Nation* warned in apocalyptic fashion that 'if the Eng-lish influx continues at the present rate the very existence of Kernow, the Cornish homeland is under threat as a cultural, national entity'.[5] In the face of such traumatic change a sense of anger, desperation and even panic emerged in some quarters. By early 1973, there was open talk of a physical force option, proposals to form a shadow government and to make contingency plans for take-over in the name of the Cornish people in the event of civil breakdown. An increasingly fevered British political environment compounded Cornish concerns over property speculation and the effects of migration. Inflation and unemployment were both ris-ing rapidly, the trade unions were confronting the Tory Government, Northern Ireland had erupted into violence and oil prices were set to quadruple as the long post-war boom faltered. The years of political consensus and economic growth seemed at an end.

The tone of *Cornish Nation* became more strident and complaints began to surface about its increasingly sympathetic coverage of Irish Republicanism. One long-standing member was claiming in a letter in 1973 that 'attempts to view conditions in Cornwall in Irish terms do grave disservice to the Celtic cause in Cornwall'.[6] At the same time its editorials were accused by readers of being too anti-English. But even the NEC in the summer of 1973 was issuing press releases claiming that unless there was remedial action, 'the desperate housing and economic situation in Cornwall may soon give rise to civil unrest'. The volatile atmosphere was not helped by accusations in the *Sunday Independent* that MK mem-bers were having their phones tapped and letters opened, or (unproven) rumours of telephone wires being cut and petrol bombs thrown. And, in 1974, the predictable press release emerged from the 'Free Cornish Army', enclosing a photo of its volunteers in training and claiming '40 fully trained units'.[7] The 'volunteers' turned out to be Plymouth Polytechnic students who had managed to dupe both the local media and politicians.[8] But the very fact that a lot of people were so easily taken in speaks volumes about the atmosphere of the time.

At this time of crisis and in the face of seemingly unstoppable forces that appeared to threaten the very existence of the Cornish nation a minority of people wanted to turn inwards and confine themselves to a very exclusive brand of ethnic nationalism. At the 1973 AGM an attempt to restrict membership to people who could 'prove Cornish birth with family trees going back through several centuries' was defeated after being condemned as being racialist.[9] This issue of 'racialism' was further complicated by the growth of racist sentiment in England. Its impact was first visible during the overspill debates when some letter writers clearly jumped on the anti-overspill bandwagon in order to express fears about the migration of people of New Commonwealth origins to Cornwall. Such comments were seized upon by opponents of MK and used to question the motives of nationalists. An undertow of colour-based racism remained into the 1970s and some of the bitter cartoons that appeared at this time in *Cornish Nation* could well be interpreted in this light. But the core of the MK leadership, those having a more sophisticated 'Celtic national-ist' ideological perspective, were colour-blind. They refused to pander to the sub-stratum of racist views being fostered at this time by the dis-course of some elements of the London tabloid press. Nevertheless, there remained a small minority of individuals who could be attracted to both MK *and* to the far right English/British nationalist parties in the 1970s and 1980s. This confusion to some extent reflected a less devel-oped political philosophy of Cornish nationalism but was also a symp-tom of a lack of 'Cornishness' in local schooling and the absence of institutions that could engender a positive and confident sense of civic consciousness in Cornwall.

In this crucial period, despite the considerable pressures on it, MK resisted the temptation to fall back onto a defensive ethnic nationalism and instead committed itself to a process that was more inclusive. At the same time as physical force options and demands for ethnic purity were being resisted on the one side, there were calls on the other for MK to revert to being a cultural pressure group.[10] This too was rejected. Len Truran argued forcefully in *Cornish Nation* for a combination of cultural, political and economic nationalism.[11] Nevertheless, the balancing act required to maintain a constitutional, democratic and political path was becoming increasingly precarious as 1973 gave way to 1974.

Problems reached a head in that year. In September 1974, amongst the unexceptional content about culture, music and sport, *Cornish Nation* published a photo of the dead Irish hunger striker, Michael Gaughan, describing him as a 'Celtic hero'.[12] The mainstream local press took time to pick the story up but in late November it was splashed in the midst of an IRA bombing campaign in the English midlands. This triggered a press statement from MK's officers rejecting 'the extreme views' of the September issue of *Cornish Nation* and apologising for any offence it might have caused. In January 1975 an emergency general meeting broadened the editorial board but allowed James Whetter to stay as editor. 'Deep disagreements' were supposedly 'healed' and MK and the *Cornish Nation* were now both committed to constitutional action'.[13] The disagreements were only patched over, however, not healed.

The 1974 elections

In the meantime there had been elections to fight. In February of 1974 Ted Heath called a snap election during a miners' strike. Taken unawares, MK decided the three week campaign was insufficient to fight the Falmouth-Camborne constituency again, as was the original intention. However, in Truro James Whetter went ahead as official candidate. His platform called for an end to the 'unhealthy dependence' on tourism, and for better housing, wages and incomes, while pledging to look after the interests of the Cornish people, appealing to 'kith and kin'. His vote of 850 was 1.5 per cent of the total and not hugely dissimilar to that of Richard Jenkin in neighbouring Falmouth-Camborne four years earlier. However, there was no hint in Cornwall of any echo of the large surge in the nationalist vote in Scotland and Wales. The groundwork – in terms of local organisation and local election candidates – had just not been done. Despite a network of branches, there was neither effective electoral machinery nor sufficient energy to build it. Although some members (for example at Penzance, Hayle, Padstow) had stood without the party label, the lack of official MK local government candidates between 1971–1975 meant a parallel lack of public visibility for the organisation.

The period between 1970 and 1974 had thus been a crucial one. In Wales the years from 1959–66 had laid the foundations for some electoral success.[14] The momentum begun then continued through to 1974 when Plaid won two seats in February and three in October. By being positioned as the main challengers to Labour in several seats Plaid Cymru was able to capitalise in 1974 on the general disaffection from the two largest London parties. This was even more the case in Scotland, where the SNP made a spectacular breakthrough in the 1974 elections, having displaced the Liberals as third party over most of Lowland Scotland during the 1960s and 1970s. In Cornwall, in contrast, MK's shift to electioneering in the late 1960s had been hesitant and unconvincing. This ambivalence about whether to contest elections and MK's relatively late entry into the electoral arena coincided with the survival and revival of the Liberal Party in Cornwall in the 1950s and 1960s. MK's failure to establish itself as an electoral alternative in the 1960s and early 1970s meant the Liberals had free rein and could build from their existing electoral base in east Cornwall, where they had won both Parliamentary seats in 1966. By 1974 the Liberals were much more visible in Cornwall than in large parts of Wales and Scotland. In consequence they were neatly placed to sweep up what anti-metropolitanism existed, capitalising also on popular disillusion with Heath's Tories and Wilson's Labour Party.

In the second election of October 1974 James Whetter again stood for MK in Truro and this time felt the full force of the swing to the Liberals. His vote was mercilessly squeezed to a mere 384 or 0.7 per cent of the total. The Liberal Party's David Penhaligon, playing the patriotic Cornish card, succeeded in ousting the Conservatives. Even some MK members preferred to work for the Liberals, while the prediction in *Cornish Nation* that the Liberal vote 'will be dissipated as quickly as it arose' proved to be hopelessly wide of the mark.[15] MK's love-hate relationship with the Liberals had again returned to haunt it, and not for the last time. In 1968 some Liberals had suggested an electoral alliance, and yet in the same year Jeremy Thorpe called for a regional assembly based on Cornwall, Devon and Somerset. The Liberal Party in Cornwall was able to hunt with the hounds and run with the fox. They supported measures of self-government when it suited them at the same time as their colleagues in Devon were aggressively demanding the amalgamation of Cornish and Devon institutions.[16] In doing so they remained flexible enough to sideline MK in the 1970s and retain their traditional Cornish base of voting support, something they found more difficult to achieve in large parts of Scotland and Wales.

In the face of resurgent Liberalism, Falmouth-Camborne constituency adopted a different stance in the October 1974 election. Rather than confront the Liberals directly it was decided to support Jon Davey, former Liberal candidate in 1970, but now running as an Independent Liberal. In the end Davey won 2,246 votes (4.4 per cent). This strategy was defended by Len Truran on the grounds that 'we must seek to occupy the radical middle ground that they (the Liberals) once occupied ... we must espouse causes that they would wish to champion and we must out-think them in radical policies'.[17] Given that many 'patriotic' Cornish voters cast their votes for the Liberals this was a logical and perceptive strategy but given also the strength and flexibility of the Liberals in

Cornwall, it is less easy to see how they could be displaced from this shared 'radical middle' ground. Furthermore, by supporting Independent Liberals rather than standing their own candidates, MK if anything increased confusion amongst the average voters about where Liberalism ended and Cornish nationalism began.

Stannary Parliament and the second CNP

In any case the tensions within MK seemed set to blow the organisation apart. The 1975 AGM saw an unsuccessful attempt to oppose the existing leadership.[18] This was linked to a new source of tension in the reappearance of the Stannary Parliament, revived in early 1974 after protests over a Pay Board rejection of a wage rise for china clay workers. Some nationalists in mid-Cornwall argued that the legal privileges given to the Cornish Stannaries in a series of royal charters since 1201 were still constitutionally valid. In particular they pointed to Henry VII's Charter of Pardon of 1508, which confirmed the right of a Stannary Parliament to represent Cornwall's tinners and extended its power further by giving it certain rights of veto.[19] The original Stannary Parliament had gradually fallen into disuse, last meeting in 1752, by which time it had fallen into the hands of an unrepresentative clique of gentry and merchants. Nevertheless in 1974 its claims were dusted off and re-stated. The Duchy establishment studiously ignored demands to recall it in order to discuss the Pay Board decision so a small group of activists unilaterally reconvened it.

The appearance of the Stannary Parliament and its account of Cornwall's constitutional rights was a powerful draw for many in MK and posed a dilemma for others. It had become palpably clear by 1974 that MK was in for a long struggle if it was to gain electoral acceptance. The possibility of a shortcut to devolution was a tempting one and the single-mindedness with which Brian Hambly had led the reconvening of the House of Stannators impressed many MK members and contrasted with MK's own vacillations in the early 1970s. If Cornwall already had its legitimate law making body based on its ancient constitutional rights then why struggle to convince a stubborn London Government of the need to reform its jealously guarded centralised system? Even for others, who were aware that it was one thing to recover lost rights and another thing altogether to convince the populace to act on them, there was a dilemma. What should MK's position be in relation to the Stannary Parliament? While there were those who wished the movement to recognise the Stannary Parliament as Cornwall's legitimate governing body, others preferred to stay well clear of it. Confusion was compounded by the local press, which tended to treat MK and Stannary interchangeably. Thus, when Donald Rawe claimed exemption from paying road tax under Stannary law at Launceston's magistrates court he was described as 'MK chief' rather than Stannary activist.[20]

The Stannary Parliament appealed perhaps most strongly to those who adopted a nostalgic approach to Cornish politics. As an example of this Edward Trewin-Wolle, a Stannary sympathiser in 1975, had previously argued in his local election leaflet of 1970 at Falmouth that MK was 'dedicated to preserving Cornwall intact for future generations; the heritage, its beautiful mysterious land, its customs, privileges, lore and language. The movement is democratic, open and loyal to our Queen'. While the appeal of the Stannary to legitimate rights resonated strongly with a certain loyalist strand of opinion within MK, others saw it, in contrast, as 'nothing but delusion and disappointment', 'speculative and irrelevant', 'romantic day dreaming' and out of touch with 'a sense of practical political reality'.[21] In the end, the May 1975 AGM narrowly rebuffed what some viewed as an attempt by one or two stannators together with James Whetter to 'take over', although the 'margin of victory was small'.[22] This was a victory possibly made easier by the way Stannary proceedings had rapidly turned to farce in early 1975 when leading activist Fred Trull was suspended by an emergency meeting of the Stannary Parliament after his Oxfordshire birthplace was revealed in a local newspaper.[23] This also set the tone for the Stannary's continuing commitment to an ethnic, as opposed to civic, nationalism.

After his defeat in the AGM election for Chairman James Whetter soon resigned to form the Cornish Nationalist Party. In leaving, he called for a greater politicisation of the party; 'MK was not equipped to become a positive nationalist movement'.[24] He declared the CNP would look to an all-embracing electoral strategy, but, other than this greater emphasis on electioneering, the CNP's aims were actually remarkably close to those of MK. One difference was that the CNP was, at first, a pro-European party, affiliating itself to the European Federalist Party and forging links with groups throughout Europe. In spite of its stated aims the CNP found it no easier to contest elections than had MK. In its early days it had three prospective parliamentary candidates lined up in Peter Flamank in Bodmin and then North Cornwall, Pedyr Prior at St. Ives and James Whetter still at Truro. But Pedyr Prior publicly defected to MK in 1976 and, eventually, only James Whetter was left to stand in the 1979 General Election (winning just 227 votes).

Before this election the CNP had suffered some adverse, and in the long run fatal, publicity. In December 1976 MK was somewhat surprised to learn that, for the CNP, it was 'public enemy No 1', 'quislings' and 'dolls in the hands of the Westminster Government'. The CNP was intending to 'take steps to eliminate' MK.[25] In contrast, it was the CNP who were as good as eliminated by the fallout from its plans for a 'Greenshirts' youth wing. For news had surfaced that the energetic CNP organiser in West Cornwall was intending to form a uniformed youth wing. The local press leapt upon the 'Greenshirts' issue with alacrity. After some hesitation the CNP was forced to disown the more extremist statements associated with the project, while in January 1977 the Stannary Parliament stepped in to order the CNP to call off a promised Greenshirts march in Camborne. This episode effectively marginalised the CNP and by early 1977 MK was claiming that the CNP was a 'small, insignificant group'.[26] The Greenshirts rapidly disappeared into nationalist folklore. Later that year it was reported that its founder had left the CNP because of its 'infiltration by communist elements' and was on the verge of joining the National Front.[27]

A phoenix arises

Unfortunately for the CNP, its electoral strategy was undermined by an influx of younger members into MK in the mid-1970s. Lacking roots in MK's pressure group past or memories of it, these new members, as we shall see, pressed MK into a more overt electoral strategy. Just as the CNP began to contest elections the re-emergence of MK as a political force soon pushed the CNP into playing a relatively minor role. Indeed, like a phoenix, MK surprisingly quickly recovered from the ashes of the 1975 split. Within four years it was mounting its most successful electoral intervention to date, having surmounted the challenge posed by the appearance of the Stannary Parliament and the second CNP.

It may seem odd that the uninspiring election results of 1974 and the split of 1975 were accompanied by an influx into MK of a younger generation of activists. They were predominantly in their 20s and most had spent various periods of time away from Cornwall working or at university. They had also been influenced as much by the general upsurge in Celtic nationalism of the early 1970s as by the various 'threats' to Cornwall that had so exercised the movement in the early 1970s. At the same time, at the end of 1974, MK's secretary Len Truran had formed the An Gof Group, an internal campaigning body of active members which aimed to match the energy of the exile-based Cowethas Flamank. This small and shifting group of activists commenced a steady stream of press releases and letters, establishing a much more consistent pattern of publicity for MK. Other voices, most notably Bert Boyd at Illogan, were calling for MK to 'take the lead and organise itself politically' in order to become a 'proper' political party.[28] MK, he urged, needed a 'complete change of direction ... to take advantage of coming problems of unemployment, wages, prices, housing'.[29] And this is exactly what happened.

In March 1975 Richard Jenkin made a statement that MK hoped to contest every General Election seat. To do this it intended to form constituency associations, something that slowly emerged over the next two or three years. If anything, the departure of James Whetter and the formation of the CNP in the summer of 1975 spurred on this development and in February 1976 Len Truran was duly adopted as prospective parliamentary candidate at St. Ives. By April candidates were in place in Falmouth-Camborne (Richard Jenkin) and Bodmin (Michael Payne-Jago). Truro and North Cornwall were left to the CNP in a tacit and unspoken electoral agreement. A year later there was a switch when Richard Jenkin resigned as candidate in Falmouth-Camborne. Len Truran moved over to this constituency and Colin Murley was adopted in his place at St. Ives. In the meantime at Bodmin Roger Holmes had replaced Michael Payne-Jago, who during his time as candidate had generated some no-holds barred press releases, in 1976 for example calling for 'complete independence' in a speech to MK's London branch.[30]

All three constituencies to be fought by MK therefore had local candidates in place more than two years before the eventual election. The movement now seemed more set for the electoral arena than it had been previously. It had chosen its path of 'constitutional, peaceful and democratic action'.[31] According to the April issue of *Forward* 'we have now taken the first step in the fight to free ourselves from the humiliating dependence upon handouts from the country that has robbed us of our birthright. It will neither be a short fight nor an easy one … we may lose time and time again but if we stick it out, we shall win'.[32] At the Spring Conference of 1976 the ambiguous political position of MK was further clarified when a resolution was carried almost unanimously to exclude members of other parties. (Before this time only NEC members could not hold dual membership). The momentum was clearly towards a separate and distinct political identity, although at subsequent AGMs into the 1980s an older generation of members could still occasionally be heard questioning whether MK was a political party or not.

New issues

By late 1975 the growing economic problems of the British state were beginning to impinge seriously on Cornwall as global economic difficulties finally reached the Tamar. The jobs and land speculation boom of the early 1970s had collapsed, Keynesian economic management faltered and unemployment begun a remorseless upwards rise. MK press releases at this time were a mixture of old issues – continuing to snipe at Plymouth's attempts to encroach on the border and expand its influence in Caradon – and new issues, such as unemployment, the abuse of the key worker scheme, second homes or the threat posed by heavily capitalised Scottish boats to the mackerel fishery. Together with new issues a more innovative approach can be discerned. For example, MK produced a 'certificate of Cornish nationality' to back its campaign for maternity facilities in east Cornwall, neatly combining an issue of health resources with a cultural appeal to Cornish identity. In this way it combined the role of political party with pressure group activity, tying the visible campaigning of the 1960s into the electoral politics that were to become more typical of the 1990s. This campaigning style was tested in the district and county council elections of 1976 and 1977. The number of candidates again slowly rose as MK entered its second electoral phase. Six members stood under the official label in 1976, in which year Neil Plummer was successful at Stithians and Roger Holmes at Liskeard, the first MK success in local authority elections since 1969. In 1977 seven candidates stood for Cornwall County Council, from St. Ives in the west to Liskeard in the east, achieving an encouraging mean percentage vote of 17.1 per cent. By now it was no surprise that the *West Briton* chose to comment that 'none of … the fringe parties – including MK … did very well'.[33]

At the same time MK was moving towards a more clearly articulated left of centre position. Much has occasionally been made of the left-right divisions within MK at this time. But in Cornish nationalist politics there was always a tendency to use such descriptions as elements of political name-calling and personal in-fighting rather than as accurate accounts of political positions. Thus, on the CNP's departure in 1975, it was quickly caricatured by some MK activists as 'Marxist-Leninist'.[34] Again in 1980 there was a lot of talk of Trotskyites and 'members of the Socialist Workers Party'. None of these descriptions bore much resemblance to the truth. It was the case that from the early 1970s some MK members openly espoused a socialist position, but this was an echo of what was by the 1970s a fashionable position in the other Celtic countries. In 1978 a loose group emerged in MK around the magazine *An Weryn*[35] arguing for an explicit decentralist socialism, influenced not by Trotsky but by libertarian socialism as well as the leftism of the Union Democratique Bretonne (UDB). But there was no great gap between the positions of the *An Weryn* group and the mainstream MK line at this time – 'a caring policy aimed at correcting past neglects and giving Cornwall the right to make its own decisions here in Cornwall'.[36]

Certain issues could, however, still be the cause of much internal debate. One of these in the late 1970s was MK's attitude to the British monarchy. The poorly attended Spring Conference of 1977 voted by two to one to call for the Duchy's lands in Cornwall to be restored to a democratically elected Cornish Assembly. This was perhaps predictably met by 'shock-horror' headlines in the local press along the lines of 'MK says strip the Duke of his land'. More crucially, it also confronted the strong loyalist tradition of an older generation of MK members. As an example, when MK's memorial to the 'rebels' of 1497 was originally unveiled at St. Keverne in October 1966 it had somewhat ironically been accompanied by prayers 'for the Queen and those in authority'.[37] From the same era, MK's 1970 general election manifesto publications stressed that the movement was 'loyal to Her Majesty'. For several of the newer generation of MK activists such British loyalism was incompatible with Cornish nationalism. Nonetheless, loyalist sentiment was still strong enough in 1977 for the June AGM to vote by more than two to one to send a letter of congratulations to the Queen on her jubilee, albeit written in Cornish!

While differences remained between monarchists and republicans, MK activists, whether 'left' or 'right', were united in 1977 in opposition to key worker policies and in calling for the right to work for Cornish workers. The party also took a lead in opposing nuclear dumping in Cornwall. Its growing environmentalist stance resulted in Teddy Goldsmith, the prospective Ecology Party candidate in Falmouth-Camborne, withdrawing in favour of MK's Len Truran. Furthermore, MK members began to take to the streets in this period and adopt a greater public visibility. In October 1977, as unemployment rates soared to more than 12 per cent, MK's Len Truran joined the Labour Party's PPC in Falmouth-Camborne on the platform at a public rally against unemployment at Pool. In December 1978 and January 1979 MK held its own rallies at Penzance and Falmouth in support of the Cornish fishing industry, calling for a 50 mile exclusion zone for Cornish boats. And in March 1979 in a more cultural manifestation of Cornishness, local MK members organised the first St. Piran's Day rally at Truro.

Modest success – the 1979 elections

In late 1978 Len Truran eloquently summed up the reasons why people should vote for MK. He said it was a:

> progressive party with a policy for Cornwall and a vested inter-est in seeing that Cornwall is its first concern. It must be a vote that is *for* the survival of Cornwall, the Cornish, our way of life, traditions and prosperity. It must be a vote *against* the continu-ing colonial treatment of Cornwall – for we are England's old-est colony, suffering from the chronic effects of that colonisation'.[38]

In May 1979 many people did choose to vote MK. The party polled 1,662 votes (4.0 per cent) in St. Ives, 1,637 (3.0 per cent) in Falmouth-Camborne and 865 (1.7 per cent) in Bodmin. Although activists were disappointed it was not higher, the St. Ives result was higher in percentage terms than Plaid Cymru's performance in 14 of the 36 Welsh constituencies, the Falmouth-Camborne result higher than 12 and even the Bodmin result better than Plaid's at Monmouth, Newport and Cardiff South East. These results and the over 9,000 votes cast for a record 19 candidates at the district council elections, a number not surpassed until 1999, seemed to mark a coming of age. While the SNP and Plaid Cymru had slipped back from their peak of 1974 MK had built considerably in a difficult year for third and fourth parties when attention was focused on the 'winter of discontent' and the battle between Callaghan and Thatcher.

How might we explain this modest success? As noted above MK had three local and well-known candidates in place early. They were backed up by regular press releases and, from the spring of 1978, there was considerable canvassing. Supplementing this were some less conventional activities, like the Gwary Myr festival at St. Just in 1978 which gave the organisation extra publicity. Solid groundwork had been laid. Indeed, it is possible that Callaghan's delayed calling of the election had an adverse effect on MK's vote. Expecting an election in the autumn of 1978 MK may have peaked too early. Moreover, the feeling from canvassers in 1979 was that, at the last moment, there was a considerable swing, at least in Falmouth-Camborne, back to the Liberals as MK sympathisers resorted to a more familiar option. This may be indicated in the fact that while 1,637 people voted for MK in the Parliamentary election over 4,500 had cast a vote for MK in the local elections held on the same day in that constituency. In addition, the focus of MK electioneering in the late 1970s, in St. Ives especially on a fiercely anti-Tory platform, may have had the effect of consolidating Liberal/Labour votes against the Conservatives, while making it more difficult to win over Tory voters.

It could be argued that the real legacy of the hard work put in before the 1979 elections was felt in the election to the European Parliament that closely followed the General Election. With less pressure to vote tactically 10,205 people cast their votes for MK's Richard Jenkin. MK had consistently called for a revised European constituency that recognised Cornwall as one unit but the eventual placing of Plymouth in a combined Cornwall and Plymouth constituency focused attention on the old enemy across the Tamar and raised the emotive issue of Cornish integrity. In this election as much as 9 or 10 per cent of the Cornish vote went to MK, indicating its potential. Yet the irony of this was that the decision to contest the Euro-election was only taken after a protracted and finely balanced internal debate. MK had opposed the entry into the EEC in 1975 on the grounds that the terms would irreparably harm the interests of producers in Cornwall, especially small farmers and the fishing industry. Opposition to the EEC remained strong through 1977 and 1978. Consequently, when St. Ives Constituency proposed to the December 1978 NEC that the party contest the Euro-election there were considerable doubts. Some felt that it was a distraction from the parliamentary elections, others were concerned about the cost and yet others opposed it in principle, calling for an 'active boycott'.[39] A resolution to leave the matter on the table was only rejected on the chairman's casting vote while the motion to contest in principle slipped through by 14 votes to 10 after a long discussion. It wasn't until March of 1979 that it was finally decided to stand Richard Jenkin as MK's Euro-election candidate. If an earlier, more enthusiastic, decision had been taken about this election and more resources diverted to it, it is quite possible that the result would have been even more impressive.

Post-election blues

Immediately after the General Election *Cornish Nation* pointed out that 'in the past, MK has suffered splintering and attack from those who have had no patience with our decision to build on sound foundations'.[40] However, the *Cornish Nation* editorial writer was being somewhat over-optimistic as similar divisions were about to recur as simmering internal tensions again mounted. Squabbles over MK's complex financial arrangements had emerged as early as the autumn of 1978. The elections of 1979 provided an alternative focus but, late in that year, issues of accountability and transparency re-surfaced. These were compounded by disputes over attitudes to the umbrella 'Cornish Assembly' that had been formed in May 1979 at Bodmin.[41] Meanwhile, local disagreements in Camborne had led to a short-lived breakaway Roskear branch emerging as an alternative to the existing branch.

The lack of trust that accompanied these events were compounded by ongoing debates about the policy and direction of the party. After the election the left in the party began to push for a more efficient constitution and a more decentralised organisational structure but the debate was soon mired in growing personal disputes. Tensions came to a head at the delayed AGM of October 1979 at Truro. Pedyr Prior (see Appendix) was proposed as Secretary in opposition to Len Truran. The vote went to Len, but it was relatively close, 53–40. In any case it proved a pyrrhic victory for the Secretary, who now faced a NEC which, by this time, was having difficulties finding common ground with him. In May 1980 Len Truran, who had played a major role in keeping MK on a constitutional, democratic and progressive path since 1968, finally resigned from the post of Secretary and from the NEC.

This was a serious loss to the party, but it was exacerbated when he then followed up his resignation by an attack on 'extremists' in MK, citing as an example a resolution passed at the January Policy Conference in favour of a 'phased closure of military bases'.[42] Both the resolution and the later press coverage was stimulated by the renewed Cold War and anti-communist atmosphere being generated by the rightwards lurch in British and American politics. MK was suddenly receiving major, though unwanted, publicity. Both the *Daily Telegraph* and the *Guardian* in June carried highly coloured stories of 'long in the tooth revolutionaries' and 'reds' who were blighting the 'Cornish dawn'.[43] True to form, press releases from both MK and from those accused of subversion in the *An Weryn* group went unpublished outside Cornwall. The upshot of the 1980 'troubles' was a rash of resignations from MK. These included some of those, on both sides, who had been active in the run up to the 1979 elections.

MK had therefore ended the 1970s with disillusion setting in after a poorer than anticipated election result and the loss of members following an internal dispute. But at least this time yet another splinter group had not emerged and several of those who left in 1980–1981 eventually returned. At the same time, the 1970s had also seen MK make an unambiguous transition from pressure group to political party. Moreover, its election results of 1979 can be seen, in retrospect, as the high point of the 1970s and 80s. The 1980s were to bring its own problems as Cornish nationalists struggled to carve out a space for a 'new politics' in the unsympathetic context of Thatcherite Britain.

Notes

1. *Kevren*, 1 (1971). *Kevren*, the magazine produced by the Cowethas Flamank, continued into the 1980s. Begun as a research and information provider to MK, by 1976 *Kevren* was distancing itself from MK and providing information to 'any bonafide Cornish organisation' (*Kevren* 17 (1976)).
2. MK press release, 11 April 1970, MK Collection
3. *Cornish Nation*, Vol. 2, 5 (September 1971).
4. *Camborne Packet*, 27 September 1972.
5. *Cornish Nation*, Vol. 2, 13 (September 1973).
6. Letter to Len Turan, March 1973, MK Collection.
7. *Sunday Independent*, 13 May 1973; *Celtic News*, October 1973 (*Celtic News* was the newsletter of the Celtic League); *Sunday Independent*, 3 March 1974.
8. *Western Morning News*, 8 March 1974.
9. *Sunday Independent*, 24 June 1973.
10. *Kevren* 5 (1973).

11. *Cornish Nation*, Vol. 2, 14 (November 1973).
12. *Cornish Nation*, Vol. 2, 17 (September 1974).
13. *Kevren* Vol. 11 (1975).
14. Linda McAllister (2001), *Plaid Cymru: The Emergence of a Political Party*, Bridgend, p. 114.
15. *Cornish Nation*, Vol. 2, 15 (March 1974).
16. See, for example, *West Briton*, 6 October 1977 and *Western Morning News*, 29 April 1977.
17. *Carn* 8 (1974). *Carn* was the monthly journal of the Celtic League, produced at first with the newsletter *Celtic News*. It is still published, containing news and comment from all the Celtic countries.
18. *Forward* (June 1975); *Cornish Nation* Vol. 3, 2 (Autumn 1975). *Forward* was a short-lived newsletter published by Bert Boyd and the Illogan Group of MK activists in 1975–76.
19. G.R.Lewis (1908), *The Stannaries: A Study of the Medieval Tin Mines of Cornwall and Devon*, Truro, p. 127.
20. *Kevren*, 14 (1975).
21. *Forward*, 4–6 (June-August 1975).
22. *Forward*, 4 (June 1975).
23. *Kevren*, 14 (1975).
24. *Cornish Banner*, 1 (1975).
25. *Cornishman*, 16 December 1976.
26. Letter from Len Truran to *Camborne Packet*, 19 January 1977, MK Collection.
27. *Western Morning News*, 30 September 1977.
28. *Forward*, 1 (March 1975).
29. Letter from Bert Boyd to Len Truran, 27 December 1975, MK Collection.
30. Press release from Michael Payne-Jago, July 1976, MK Collection.
31. *Cornish Nation*, Vol. 4, 1 (Autumn 1976).
32. *Forward*, Vol. 2, 2 (April 1976).
33. *West Briton*, 12 May 1977.
34. *Scots Independent*, September 1975.
35. *An Weryn* was an independent 'radical magazine' published by an informal editorial team which included Maggie Casson, Bernard Deacon, Maggie Johns, Paul Johns, Ian Williams, Jan Williams and Malcolm Williams.
36. Letter to members from Len Truran, 1978, MK Collection.
37. 'An Gof memorial – Order of Common Service, October 22, 1966', MK Collection.
38. *Cornish Nation*, 35 (1978).
39. Minutes of MK NEC meeting, December 1978, MK Collection.
40. *Cornish Nation*, 37 (Summer 1979).
41. This was an attempt to bring together a cross-organisation group that could campaign on Cornish issues. Led by Harry Callender of Torpoint, it survived for a decade but was regarded by many nationalists as little more than a self-selected talking shop with an ambiguous line on devolution.
42. *Cornishman*, 5 June 1980.
43. *Daily Telegraph*, 2 June 1980; *Guardian*, 3 June 1980.

VI

DECADE OF DOUBTS: 1980–1990

By the mid 1980s the deep personal rifts of 1979–80 had been, to some extent, healed. The more unfortunate aspect of this, the third split in just over a decade, was that it diverted MK from building on what hindsight reveals as genuine electoral progress in 1979. This was doubly unfortunate as it coincided with the less accommodating context of Thatcherite Britain. Instead, like the SNP and Plaid Cymru as well as the Labour Party, it entered into a period of internal reflection about its philosophy and role. In consequence, MK was, for some years after 1981, less electorally visible outside of the far west of Cornwall where it maintained a vigorous electioneering profile for a few years. It was at this time that there was a considerable shift within the Cornish movement, with many MK activists preferring to channel their enthusiasms into a range of single issue campaigns and short-lived pressure groups. A productive period in some ways for the Cornish movement, it was nonetheless a decade of doubts about the direction of overt political nationalism and by the end of the 1980s MK as a political force was a shadow of its former self.

The debates continue

The spate of resignations from Mebyon Kernow had slowed by the end of 1980, but the battle for the heart and soul of the party continued for another two to three years. The alleged infiltration of leftists into the party may have been described by the Guardian as a 'tribute to the relative vitality of Mebyon Kernow',[1] but the 'vibrant' internal party debates were gradually sapping the enthusiasm and morale of a range of activists, worn down by the constant meetings and manoeuvrings. There were broadly two positions in this debate. For traditionalists it was essential that MK continued to be a broad-based party that could potentially attract the support of all people in Cornwall whether they were right or left. This implied emphasising the 'Cornish' and 'nationalist' parts of the message and leaving MK's position on social and economic matters vague. Thus, Richard Jenkin continued to call for MK not to restrict its appeal in any way. Describing himself as a 'flag-waving, libertarian, Cornish patriot' he told an MK conference in 1981, 'the vision we founder-members had of Mebyon Kernow was of an organisation which could be supported by all Cornish people who recognised the national identity of Cornwall …'[2]

A number of the younger members of MK did not agree. They saw what they viewed as woolliness on the bread and butter issues that mattered to ordinary voters as leading to an inability either to enthuse the electorate or to garner their votes. In 1981, they formed the Cowethas 1913 group within the party. Named after the unsuccessful strike of clay workers in the St. Austell area in 1913, it was founded on the three principles of autonomy, socialism and ecology, arguing that 'true national liberation for Cornwall is impossible without a social revolution to bring the commanding heights of the economy under the control of the people of Cornwall'.[3] While comparisons can be made with the socialist National Left grouping in Plaid Cymru and the subsequently proscribed '79 Group in the SNP, many of the founding sentiments of the 1913 Group were more acutely influenced by the Breton UDB. The group wished to co-opt many of the Breton party's 'autogestionaire' ideas, which called for radical devolution to the lowest possible level, whilst also – like both the UDB and Plaid Cymru in the late 1980s – building bridges to left and green movements.

Members of the 1913 Group were not slow to criticise the traditionalists. Julyan Drew (see Appendix) argued that 'the Cornwall envisaged by many MK members and officers would make our country an ever richer crock of gold for the tourist operators and itinerant mining companies. It is not enough to seek a self-governing Cornwall and then to work for economic and social justice. The two must go hand in hand'.[4] Likewise Malcolm Williams maintained that the decline in membership since 1979 was, in fact, to MK's advantage. He claimed; 'MK needed to shed its surplus flesh, after all it's been going through a revolutionary process – the actual loss of membership has been small – retired colonels and elements of the county set'.[5] The public flashpoints of the internal debate between 1980 and 1982 remained the various Policy Conferences. As before, the usual host of motions dear to MK hearts – a more constructive tourist industry, Cornish identity, distinctive labelling of local produce – sailed through virtually unanimously. But in an increasing number of areas, such as defence, the monarchy and public ownership, the debates divided the party. The areas of disagreement were rehearsed frequently during this period, with the party's official position changing on a regular and, to outsiders, somewhat confusing basis. Sometimes this even occurred from one conference to the next, depending on the balance of attendance. In February 1981, for example, the party passed a motion calling for the 'closure of foreign military bases in Cornwall' a motion very similar to that condemned by Len Truran in 1980. This was again supported at an April AGM but at the Perranporth Policy Conference of November 1981 it was overturned on a two to one vote. The Perranporth Conference did however finally commit Mebyon Kernow to a republican stance, but a further motion calling for the 'Cornish people's eventual ownership of the creation and distribution of wealth', was easily defeated by three to one.

The St. Austell Conference of November 1982 has been widely credited as the meeting which 'pulled the party back from the brink, avoiding the political schisms and divisions of the previous two years'.[6] However, many felt this was due more to the impending General and district council elections. 'Election years concentrate the mind wonderfully' is how one delegate put it. The meeting agreed a comprehensive set of economic proposals including support for co-operatives, small businesses and a considerable redistribution of wealth. Proposals for a defence policy were referred back to a policy committee, while the party's position on the monarchy was, by almost general agreement, put into 'cold storage', for a future self-governing Cornwall to decide. This end to the more fractious nature of the party's internal debate also largely coincided with the demise of the magazines, including *Cornish Nation* (later to be relaunched), *Gwyn ha Du* and *An Weryn*, through which much of the debate had been conducted. Throughout this formative period, Richard Jenkin had retained the leadership of the party and provided a sense of continuity with the earlier decades. But, while the younger activists failed to turn the party into a vehicle for their own brand of 'radical autonomism', the early 1980s had, however, consolidated MK as a progressive, left-of-centre political party. This identity first adopted in the late 1970s, has been retained by the party to the present day.

Within the uncertain political environment of this time, an unusual exception to the normally constitutional nationalism of Cornwall came in December 1980, when a bomb exploded at the courthouse in St. Austell, the scene of previous confrontations between members of the Stannary Parliament and Her Majesty's Judiciary. Responsibility was claimed by a shadowy and little known group which called itself An Gof 1980. In a telephone call to the *West Briton* newspaper, a spokesman stated that 'the attacks will continue. The An Gof movement have [*sic*] done this. People to be smashed are councillors and communist infiltrators – the ones who tried to corrupt the Cornish scene with their Muscovite tendencies will really need to sweat'.[7] At a time of rising Cold War tension, some individuals clearly managed to combine a Cornish nationalist agenda with a ferocious anti-communist bent. The action was quickly condemned by all other groups within the wider Cornish movement. MK Chairman Richard Jenkin labelled the group as a 'hindrance to the cause of Cornwall's nationality' describing them as 'anti-Cornish vandals, not nationalists'.[8]

An Gof 1980, or people claiming to be members of such an organisation, made a number of calls to local newspapers in 1980 and 1981 promising acts of political violence. They informed journalists at the *Cornishman* newspaper that they had weapons and claimed responsibility for a blaze at a Penzance hairdresser's (attacked in mistake for the Bristol and West Building Society) in January 1981. However, An Gof 1980 spent as much time threatening the left within and outside MK as they did any forces of 'English Imperialism'. Their weapons would be used against 'people not fit to lead a nationalist movement'. Late night, blood-curdling and anonymous telephone calls became a regular staple of Cornish nationalist politics at this time and MK National Secretary Pedyr Prior was telephoned and told to resign from MK 'with all your Trotskyist friends' within a month or face the consequences. A number of people who had already left MK were also contacted and told to leave the organisation, suggesting the phone-callers were not totally up to date on developments inside the party.

The promised intensification of bombings never occurred and An Gof 1980 largely disappeared from view after 1981. Later in the decade, An Gof claimed responsibility for a number of fires, including one at the Zodiac Bingo Hall in Redruth and an attempted explosion at Beacon Village Hall. The group also claimed to have deliberately placed broken glass beneath the sand of Portreath Beach in 1984. The particular rationale for these targets was always difficult to discern and the actual involvement of nationalists in the fires was never proven. An Gof re-surfaced as late as 1987, when it threatened 'revenge' on all people working on the redevelopment of the Holmans building in Camborne, its hand-written press statement demanding 'Cornish Factories – *not* Tesco's'.[9] In addition, at various times throughout the 1980s the graffiti 'An Gof' appeared at numerous places, especially in the Camborne-Redruth district. The label became synonymous with the threat of violent action and was available to anyone who wanted to cause a shudder or two in the local print media. The sensationalist instincts of the latter could always be counted on to provide some publicity, at the same time as they resisted any tendency to analyse the more mainstream Cornish national movement or the political positions it advanced.

Protests and a shift to the west

In spite of the seemingly endemic upheavals in the Cornish movement at this time, MK was able, at least for a short period, to develop a much keener and more pro-active edge to its campaigning. In 1980 and 1981 the party took the lead in protests against the impact on Cornwall and its people of the New Right policies of the Thatcher government. Taking the dramatic rise in unemployment as one of its main concerns, many of the party's younger members took to the streets – MPs were lobbied, protest rallies organised and thousands of leaflets distributed at Cornish Job Centres. Tory Party offices in Cornwall and even No 10 Downing Street were picketed. Also at this time, MK took a principal role in the campaign against the siting of a nuclear power station in Cornwall. The campaign began in the autumn of 1979, when the Atomic Energy Authority set out to explore the feasibility of constructing a new nuclear power station in the south west, with possible sites identified at Luxulyan, Gwithian and Nancekuke, near the then chemical and biological warfare plant. MK immediately condemned the plans for test drilling at Luxulyan and, by January 1980, the party had sponsored a meeting in the City Hall, Truro, to galvanise opposition, following a short burst of press activity and leafleting in the streets of the Cornish capital. A 'rainbow alliance' was formed to fight the proposals, taking much of its inspiration from similar campaigns in Brittany against nuclear power stations at Plogoff and Le Pellerin. Solidarity between the campaigns relied almost solely on the connection between MK and the UDB, with Breton and Cornish activists criss-crossing the channel to support each other's demonstrations.

The campaign, by now known as the Cornish Anti-Nuclear Alliance (CANA), took off with the usual round of protest meetings, while the people of Luxulyan followed this by spontaneously blocking local roads and taking over one of the drilling rigs. A second rig was effectively occupied by MK members and others in the wider environmentalist movement who prevented the drillers from proceeding through various non-violent tactics. The campaign grew and in July 1980 over 2,000 people attended the first of a range of rallies in Truro, addressed by a number of activists including Yves Rouger, the UDB Mayor of Concarneau, and Dora Russell, the peace campaigner. After several weeks of stand-off between protestors and the drilling companies at Luxulyan, the Central Electricity Generating Board (CEGB) declared that plans for the projected power station were cancelled. Despite CEGB denials, the protestors were convinced that this had only occurred because of the strength of public opinion. The campaign had brought together a broad coalition which included activists from most political parties. But for Cornish nationalists, their role as catalysts in making the protests happen is remembered to the

present day. Indeed, Malcolm Williams has described it as 'MK's greatest victory'. He writes 'we set ourselves a target of mobilising opinion,
building a coalition and stopping the power station. We managed to do it
and we managed to do it with a clear awareness publicly of our role'.[10] For
the first time, MK activists had also been involved closely in a campaign
with environmentalists and this heralded closer relations between MK
and the Greens in the 1980s and 1990s, even including a non-opposition
pact in the 1995 district council elections, an echo of the short-lived
electoral agreement between Plaid Cymru and the Greens in parts of
Wales in the early 1990s.

This success nonetheless coincided with a general retreat from electioneering in the early 1980s. The only part of Cornwall where the impetus of the late 1970s was maintained into the early 1980s was Penwith.
Here various activists, including Julyan Drew, Colin Lawry (see Appendix) and Malcolm Williams, for a time turned MK into one of the most
effective election-focused local campaigning forces ever seen in Cornwall. From 1980 through to about 1983, leaflets were delivered throughout Penzance and St. Just on a monthly basis, and St. Ives and the
surrounding area on a slightly less frequent basis. MK's election campaigns in these areas were also well-orchestrated and as, if not more,
professional than any of their opponents. Good results were achieved in
the 1981 County Council elections in Penzance and in 1982 Colin Lawry
won the Penzance Central ward of Penwith District Council on a platform
of 'Action on Jobs, Housing and a Nuclear-Free Penwith'. In the same
year Malcolm Williams in St. Just came a strong second. What was more
significant was that he succeeded in outpolling the newly formed Social
Democratic Party, despite the enormous media hype that had accompanied its formation.

Unfortunately for MK as a whole, the intense activity at local level in
Penwith, was not being replicated elsewhere. Put simply, the party failed
to maintain the high electoral visibility of 1979. It only contested two
seats in the General Election of 1983, when Richard Jenkin stood in
Falmouth-Camborne and Pedyr Prior in St. Ives. In both cases, votes cast
for the party fell dramatically from the 1979 level to only 582 (1.2 per cent)
and 569 (per cent) votes respectively. As far as local elections were
concerned, the picture was no less gloomy. The nine candidates MK put
forward for the 1981 Cornwall County Council elections fell to just seven
in the 1983 district council elections. As well as representing a decline in
candidate numbers, this period also demonstrated a shrinkage in the
party's geographical coverage, with all but one of the candidates contesting seats in the western districts of Kerrier and the Penwith heartland. The exception was long-standing Liskeard councillor Roger Holmes
who actually lost his district council seat in the 1983 elections.

Julyan Drew became leader of Mebyon Kernow in 1983 and, if anything, the area of electoral intervention became even smaller, restricted almost solely to West Penwith between 1984 and 1986. Colin Lawry subsequently won the Penzance South seat on Cornwall County Council in 1985, and Colin Murley also polled a strong second for MK in St. Just with over 40 per cent of the vote in a straight fight with long standing Independent and then Conservative County Councillor, J.J. Daniel. Yet although their vote held up very well in Penwith, this localised success only served to highlight the lack of activity elsewhere in Cornwall. In 1984 and 1986, other candidates continued to amass impressive votes in this area, often out-polling their Labour and SDP/Liberal Alliance opponents. For example, Penzance Town councillor Jeremy Drew narrowly missed out on election to Penwith District Council by less than 150 votes at Penzance East in 1986. These were impressive votes but the number of official party candidates was falling.

It was also during this period that the Cornish Nationalist Party had its final brush with electoral politics. In the 1983 General Election, CNP Chairman James Whetter withdrew from the Truro contest, describing Liberal MP David Penhaligon as a 'good Cornishman and a good constituency MP', before going off to fight North Cornwall. But North Cornwall provided no easier harvest of votes for the CNP which polled just 364 votes there (0.7 per cent). In 1984, James Whetter also stood in the Cornwall and Plymouth Euro-seat in a year when MK decided not to fight the election,[11] under the brave but perhaps rather unwise banner of the 'Cornish and European Federalist Party'. He polled less than 2,000 votes in the process. At local level, the CNP fought five council seats in both 1981 and 1983. Its last intervention saw two candidates in the 1985 Cornwall County Council elections at Roche and Truro, the only time the CNP contested a council seat outside of Dr Whetter's home territory of St. Austell. Since 1985, the organisation has not fought any elections at all. While the party still exists it is no longer an active political force. Dr. Whetter is still chairman and the *Cornish Banner* appears regularly, containing occasional political comment. In contrast to its earlier commitment to federalism, the CNP moved from its positions of the early 1980s and became distinctly anti-European by the end of the century, realigning itself with positions adopted by groups such as the United Kingdom Independence Party and the Countryside Movement.

A return to pressure group politics

In the mid to late 1980s, MK hit a low point in terms of its electoral interventions. The party decided not to contest any seats at the 1987

General Election, partly blaming the quadrupling of the election deposit, though the picture was just as bleak at local government level. In the same year, MK could only find two official party candidates for the 200-plus district council seats up for election. And in both 1985 and 1989, the party fought just three county council seats out of a total of 79.

While external observers were keen to document a decline in party activity, there was a discernable shift in emphasis. Building on the party's early 'direct action' initiatives such as the rallies and demonstrations in support of Cornish fishing and against unemployment in 1977–79 and the launch of CANA in 1980, the party under the leadership of Pedyr Prior (1985–1986) and Loveday Carlyon (1986–1989) (see Appendix) was seeking a strategy that saw MK as more than an electoral machine. In doing this MK was, consciously or sub-consciously, following the lead of Plaid Cymru which, in the period of Dafydd Elis Thomas's presidency from 1984 to 1991 experimented with various 'non-traditional' options.[12] Loveday Carlyon, in particular, maintained the MK tradition of promoting public debates which other political parties in Cornwall were loathe to have. In 1986, for example, she led criticism of the widespread acceptance of mass tourism as the focus for Cornwall's future economic development[13] and, following the 1987 General Election, she fronted an initiative calling for all non-Conservative parties active in Cornwall to unite in an anti-Thatcherite electoral strategy, a move that was backed by various nationalists, environmentalists and even leading Liberal Alliance members, particularly in South-East Cornwall.[14] However, as the 1987 election receded, the Liberals soon withdrew, preferring to wait ten years until the general UK-wide swing against Toryism in 1997 helped them ride to electoral victory in Cornwall.

Many MK members also re-entered the world of pressure group politics, using a range of bodies to promote their political views rather than Mebyon Kernow itself. As a result, MK's public profile contracted and membership fell away. Helping to form and run a plethora of bodies campaigning on a wide range of specific but inter-related issues, many nationalists were involved in the twice-yearly Conference on Cornwall which rapidly built a reputation as a forum for informed debate and generated a broad range of initiatives on political, constitutional, cultural and economic issues. And at the end of the decade, when the Conservatives levied the poll tax on all individuals regardless of their ability to pay, many MK members were active within the campaign against its implementation. Leading members, such as Colin Lawry, made a very public stand of non-payment while Pedyr Prior was instrumental in arranging the first anti-Poll Tax demonstration outside of Scotland. In a piece of symbolically rich theatre, an effigy of Margaret Thatcher was defeated by a young girl dressed as St. Piran in Truro's Cathedral Square before being ceremonially put to the torch.[15]

However, it was the formation of Cornish Alternatives to the Structure Plan (CASP) in 1987, which caught the public imagination with a high profile, if ultimately unsuccessful, campaign in direct response to the First Alteration of Cornwall's Structure Plan. The document tacitly accepted the view imposed by the South West Regional Planning Conference, that nearly 40,000 new houses would need to be built in Cornwall over the next 20 years, in order to 'accommodate' an associated population increase of somewhere between 65,000 and 100,000 people. This followed on from a 13.3 per cent population rise in the 1970s and an increase of over 10 per cent in the period from 1980 to 1987. Overall, the Cornish population had already increased by a third since 1961, reversing a pattern of stable or even declining numbers since 1871. Its population growth was now only exceeded by the boom counties of Cambridgeshire and Buckinghamshire. Yet, whereas those places had low unemployment, Cornwall suffered from chronic unemployment and declining wage levels. As MK had predicted during the 'overspill' debates of the 1960s, population growth was proving no easy panacea for Cornwall's economic problems. In fact, noting with dismay the construction of 'two-and-a-half new Penzances ... every decade', activists and community groups began to come together to question the established wisdom.

The first salvos in the debate led to the formation of a short-lived body called the Cornwall Concern Group, founded by John Angarrack from Bodmin. Objecting to the 'rape of Cornwall' and the desecration of the local countryside, it co-ordinated letter-writing campaigns and was responsible for widespread flyposting, followed by a comprehensive lobbying campaign. In a leaflet from 1987, MK noted that: 'the implications of this massive development and large population rise upon the stability of our communities, upon our health, education and other services and upon the environment and identity of Cornwall have not been fully understood or debated'. In an echo of the apocalyptic language of the early 1970s, the party referred to the plan as a 'Domesday Scenario for Cornwall and the Cornish' adding that 'it spells the end of both our landscape and our Cornish community as we know it'.

CASP itself was founded as a 'non-party-political group of diverse organisations and individuals' in November 1987, following the initial campaign work of MK and the Concern Group. The MK presence within CASP was very strong with Party Chairman Loveday Carlyon elected to the role of Secretary and MK councillor Roger Holmes chosen as Treasurer.[16] The group made the case that population growth did not inevitably bring about growth in local economies, especially those in a parlous state, while factors such as high unemployment and low wages were ignored by supporters of the housing increase.[17] Widespread opposition to the Plan was mobilised, though a timid and indecisive County Council failed to support calls from a minority of its councillors to reject the Plan.

The Cornish Social and Economic Research Group (CoSERG) was also formed at this time, and in 1988 produced the seminal critique *Cornwall at the Crossroads*. With the sub-title 'Living Communities or Leisure Zone?' authors Bernard Deacon, Andrew George and Ron Perry challenged the dominant assumptions about Cornwall's socio-economic future, contrasting the 'marinas, luxury yachts and millionaires' playgrounds' of the developers with the 'submerged Cornwall that refuses to go away' of poverty, low wages and high unemployment. CoSERG's proposals were to give communities a breathing space, to stop the brain drain of our dynamic young people, guarantee the right of future generations to be Cornish and retain local communities by human-scale development that respects the environment. The research and ideas of CoSERG greatly influenced the wider Cornish movement and the Cornish community as a whole, and led to another short-lived pressure group called the Cornish Declaration Group. This group distributed declarations entitled 'One and All', condemning the over-development of Cornwall and demanding devolution for Cornwall. Setting out its intention to 'challenge and offer alternatives to the media led assumptions about Cornwall's future',[18] its ten point plan was based almost entirely on the research of CoSERG. The media coverage was widespread, but both the campaign of CASP and the research of CoSERG did not penetrate far into the mindsets of decision-makers in Cornwall or London.

It was also the case that an apparent unease with the civic nationalism and the 'progressive' policies of MK and its low level of public visibility, had led to the proliferation of a number of groups or publications on the fringe of the Cornish movement around 1986–1987. All were short-lived. They included the *Free Cornwall* magazine, which launched itself as 'Cornwall's answer to Private Eye'[19] and the reactionary *An Kenethlor*,[20] published with the strapline – 'a point is reached when forbearance is no longer a virtue'. The same year saw the launch of Cornwall Against the English Rose (CATER), a grouping which campaigned against the presence of the English red rose emblem on brown tourism signs. Claiming that 'the English rose has about as much relevance to Cornwall as jellied eels, Chas and Dave or clog dancers', CATER demanded that the rose symbol be removed from local signs and threatened direct action if this did not take place. An early pamphlet stated 'If Greenpeace or CND can risk fines for the environment or world peace, then the least we can do is to risk the same for our right to be Cornish in Cornwall'. CATER's intention was to stimulate a public campaign of painting out signs in an echo of the Welsh Language Society's campaign for bilingual signs in the 1960s. However, despite canvassing the assembled Cornish bards at the 1986 Gorseth, not many members of the Cornish movement were prepared to make a public stand on the issue. It was clear that the Cornish movement had not yet generated the will to mount non-violent direct action for a strong moral cause, something that was regularly seen in Wales, where Gwynfor Evans' hunger strike had led to the creation of the Welsh Language TV channel S4C in 1981.

The Cornish branch of the Celtic League also became more active in the mid 1980s. In the absence of a meaningful MK election presence, the League went so far as to produce a Cornish Charter which it distributed in the form of a questionnaire to all candidates in the 1987 district council elections and the subsequent General Election – in an attempt to make devolution and Cornish identity an election issue. However, despite scores of press releases to all Cornwall and Plymouth-based papers and TV and radio media, publicity was virtually negligible. The lesson was drawn by some that the only way to make devolution an election issue was to fight the election.

'Devonwall'

For Cornish nationalists probably the most depressing trend of the 1980s was the renewed impetus to what they termed the 'Devonwall' process. In the 1960s, as we saw in chapter 4, there was an acceleration of the merger of Cornish public bodies into wider institutions. The Devon and Cornwall Constabulary was soon joined by South West Water, the South West Electricity Board, British Telecom and British Gas, who all treated Cornwall as only part of a larger region. From the nationalist perspective this was bad news for Cornwall for two reasons. First, it inevitably meant an export of higher level, better paid jobs, as the headquarters of these regional bodies were invariably located in Devon. This exacerbated the effect of the in-migration of thousands of relatively well-educated people competing for salaried jobs. When they arrived they found a dearth of posts to suit their qualifications and were forced into competing for less well paid jobs. This consequently worked to depress overall wage levels.

The second reason to oppose 'Devonwall' was the loss of potential control over a number of strategic utilities and industries. In the 1980s, the privatisation programme of the Tories and the greater role given to business in policy-making gave 'Devonwall' a further boost. Now privatised 'Devon and Cornwall' bodies such as South West Water were able to add their considerable financial resources to existing 'Devonwall' operations such as Westcountry TV or the *Western Morning News* to produce a powerful business and media lobby calling for 'Devonwall' based structures. A conference at Newquay in November 1987, called at the behest of the Duke of Cornwall, allowed the proponents of 'Devonwall' to come up with a proposal for a Devon and Cornwall Development Company. This was launched in January 1988, with support from Cornwall County Council, Devon County Council, Plymouth City Council, private companies and the Department of Trade and Industry, and a budget of £700,000. After its demise it was followed in the early 1990s by the Westcountry Development Corporation. This meant that, as well as the loss of jobs and decision-making, Cornwall had now lost strategic and policy-making autonomy. If this wasn't enough, it was followed by the return of regional planning dictated from Bristol, which further removed political power from Cornwall and its local authorities.

Opposition to this process, much of which proceeded quietly and well out of the public gaze, was extremely muted. Cornwall County Councillors occasionally raised doubts but these were brushed aside by calls for 'realism'. Of course, as the process unfolded and more and more institutions became 'Devonwall' ones, this so-called 'realism' gained a momentum of its own. The 'Devonwall' project became the taken-for-granted option. Moreover, key elements at the County Council had co-operated closely with the process from its earliest days. Immediately after local government re-organisation in 1973, a Joint Consultative Committee had been established by Cornwall and Devon County Councils. By the 1980s, both councils were deeply embroiled in the process of 'Devonwall', viewing this as the desired strategy for economic regeneration.

Groups like CoSERG began to point out in the late 1980s that these assumptions were fatally flawed. While benefiting certain 'Devonwall' business interests, the loss of institutions was creating a vacuum in Cornwall. CoSERG and MK were publicising the fact that far from being the solution, 'Devonwall' was actually a, perhaps even the, major problem facing Cornwall. The lack of a strong business voice in Cornwall and the rise of a branch-plant factory economy had meant that, instead of giving up Cornish based institutions the urgent need was to do the reverse. In order to balance a weak civil society in Cornwall it was necessary to build up Cornish public and public-private sector institutions that could command the tools and stimulate the thinking required to tackle Cornwall's distinctive needs, not destroy them. Developments in Europe began, by the end of the decade, to reinforce this conclusion. Cornwall County Council had set up a successful European Office in Brussels in the 1980s, one of the first in Britain. However, later, under pressure from the 'Devonwall' lobby, the Cornish Office was quietly merged into a Devon and Cornwall Office. A distinctive Cornish presence in Brussels was lost just at the time that the European Community was turning towards the concept of a Europe of the Regions and regional distinctiveness. In 1986, when the EU introduced Objective 1 funding and drew up its regional map for grant-aid purposes, the 'Devonwall' lobby ensured that Devon and Cornwall became the Level 2 region, rather than Cornwall alone, a short-sighted decision that cost millions and, as we shall see in the next chapter, later had to be reversed.

Similarly, when the Conservative Government established Training and Enterprise Councils in 1990–91, a giant Devon and Cornwall TEC was formed, despite this being the largest and most unwieldy of all the new TECs. Even a Cornish TEC would have been larger than many of the TECs that were formed at this time. Again, an opportunity to create a much-needed Cornish-based institution was lost. By the end of the 1980s, MK and others were arguing against the series of lost opportunities that were being passed up by policy-makers in Cornwall. Instead of building on Cornwall's strengths they were seemingly hell-bent on merging Cornwall into an institutional infrastructure that led to all important decisions being made by various bodies in Devon and further east. The process of 'Devonwall' was by this stage combining with the rise of the quango state to raise massive issues of democratic deficit in Cornwall.

Cornwall and Europe

One important area where MK policy gradually shifted during the 1980s was its attitude towards the European Union. The lack of a Cornish European Parliamentary constituency continued to be a principal battle-field in demands to restore the territorial integrity of Cornwall. But while this issue rumbled on in the background MK was re-thinking its broader stance on Europe. As we saw in chapter 5, MK was originally opposed to the Common Market. By 1984 the party had softened this position, demanding that 'Cornwall should have close ties to the rest of Europe' though qualifying this with the statement that the 'EEC as presently organised is a costly exercise in bureaucracy'.[21] By 1989, the party had become more positively pro-European, no doubt influenced by developments in Wales and Scotland, with the SNP adopting its 'Independence in Europe' approach. Fighting the European elections of that year, Colin Lawry called for a 'Westminster Bypass,' with the party's new manifesto arguing that 'if we can reassert our rights as one of the regions of Europe then Cornwall can have an exciting and vibrant future in an evolving Europe'.[22]

The first problem confronting this aim was the issue of representation, with Cornwall not represented directly in the European Parliament. Whitehall steadfastly refused to cede to demands for Cornwall to have its own direct links to Europe in the form of a single parliamentary seat. In 1983, MK put together a petition of over 600 people to force the Boundary Commission to hold a Local Inquiry into the matter. This was held in Plymouth in the following November and the Cornish representation was dismissed out of hand, with the Assistant Commissioner maintaining there were no 'special geographical considerations' which needed to be taken into account. In 1988, MK forced a second Local Inquiry by collecting a petition of nearly one thousand electors in less than a week. The cross-party 'Campaign for a Cornish Constituency' was set up to garner support, and grew to include Cornwall County Council, the six district councils and three of Cornwall's five MPs, as well as numerous parish councils and other bodies. The Inquiry was held at Bodmin in July 1988. This time, the Assistant Commissioner contradicted the ruling of his immediate predecessor and accepted that there were 'special geographical considerations' in relation to Cornwall, but then ruled that it would be inappropriate to give too much regard to such considerations. Cornwall was once again denied its own Euro-seat, on the grounds that it did not have enough electors to justify its own seat, even though there were fewer voters in the Highlands and Islands of Scotland seat and, pro rata, the three seats in Northern Ireland.

A party in freefall

Despite leading MK members playing important roles in a range of pressure groups and other bodies, the mid to late 1980s was a period in which Mebyon Kernow was treading water. The public profile of the party, as well as the number of activists, had declined to the point where a major crisis was in the offing. In fact, it materialised quite soon after the Euro-elections, when Loveday Carlyon resigned as MK Chair. This left the party 'in limbo' with little sense of direction and few meetings of the party's ruling National Executive taking place. The question for the 1990s was a stark one; would Cornish nationalism survive as a political force or would it wither and die?

Notes

1. *Guardian*, 3 June 1980. Also noted in *Cornish Nation* 40 (Summer 1980).
2. Speech original (undated) presented to authors.
3. Cowethas 1913 founding statement published in *Gwyn ha Du* 4 (November 1981), pp. 14–15. *Gwyn ha Du* was MK's 'political journal' edited by Malcolm Williams between 1980 and 1983. It was modelled on the UDB's Ar Falz and its motto was 'yn mes a dhathel, an desmyk' – out of argument, the answer.

4. Julyan Drew (1980) 'The Way Forward' in *Tributaries*. This was an occasional publication from the magazine *An Weryn*, which included a series of articles from activists on the future direction of the Cornish movement. Two issues appeared, the first in 1980 and the second in 1986.

5. Malcolm Williams interviewed in *An Weryn*, 18 (Spring 1982), pp. 10–11.

6. Conference report in *Gwyn ha Du*, 8 (1983), pp. 10–12.

7. *West Briton*, 11 December 1980.

8. MK press release, 12 January 1981, MK Collection.

9. *Redruth-Camborne Packet*, 8 October 1987.

10. Letter to the authors from Malcolm Williams, 1 October 2001.

11. Mebyon Kernow had selected Roger Holmes to fight the election, but later decided to withdraw his candidacy.

12. Laura McAllister (2002) *Plaid Cymru. The Emergence of a Political Party*, Bridgend, pp. 78–83.

13. *Western Morning News*, 22 September 1986.

14. Press statement released by Loveday Carlyon on behalf of a range of organisations, 16 June 1987.

15. *Kernow* 8 (April/May 1990), p. 2. This was an independent magazine published by MK members Paul Dunbar and Martyn Miller between 1989 and 1996. It is not to be confused with the magazine of the same name produced by youth members of MK in the early 1970s.

16. CASP press release, 24 November 1987.

17. See Philip Payton (1993), *Cornwall Since the War*, Exeter, p. 221.

18. *Kernow*, 5 (Oct/Nov 1989), p. 9.

19. *Free Cornwall*, 1 (May 1987). This magazine was produced by former MK member Allen Forster between 1987 and 1991.

20. Only six copies of *An Kenethlor* were produced by an editorial board which included former MK members Denzil Crowle, John Solomon and Des Mitchell.

21. MK policy booklet (1984), *Making Our Own Decisions*, Helston, p. 12.

22. MK policy booklet (1989), *The Cornish Answer*, Liskeard, p. 10.

VII

RE-AWAKENING: 1990–2002

The 1980s had ended with the party in crisis. Without a leader in place, the NEC instigated a series of meetings held throughout Cornwall during the autumn of 1989 to review the party's long-term strategy and consider the way ahead. The immediate result of this was yet another period of inactivity when no concrete proposals came forth from the meetings. MK's London Branch, frustrated by this lack of action, then took the initiative by calling an emergency meeting for April 1990. In a letter to all party members, the branch stated 'the only topic on the agenda will be whether we wish to continue as an organisation at all'. The press drew parallels with events in the Baltic countries, with the *Western Morning News* noting that 'as Eastern Europe celebrates the springtime of nationalist movements, the flower of Cornish Nationalism – Mebyon Kernow – may be wilting and could fold and die'.[1]

A small number of MK members in Cornwall, most notably Neil Plummer, chose not to participate in the emergency meeting, describing London Branch as the tail which was trying to wag the dog. Nevertheless, it went ahead – at Redruth's Murdoch House – just five minutes walk from the former hotel where MK began life back in 1951. A positive spin was put on this meeting, which was attended by many of the stalwarts of the movement, including Richard Jenkin and Len Truran, who had recently rejoined the party. Dissolution of the movement was not seriously considered; Carol Spear was elected 'acting convenor' and the party stated its clear intention to continue. Colin Lawry told the media: 'threats to Cornwall and her people are no less serious now than those at the time of the organisation's founding ... we look forward to serving the people of Cornwall'.[2] The meeting agreed to assess all options for the future direction of the party over the next three to four months. All members were consulted and the various options which came forward were presented to a further meeting, which eventually took place on 8th September.

The consultations and the September meeting predictably revisited many of the debates of the past, considering whether MK should continue as a conventional political party or revert to its 1960s status of pressure group. Others wished to discuss whether the name 'Mebyon Kernow' was any longer appropriate. Two further options were put forward. Bernard Deacon had produced a paper calling for the re-launching of MK as a 'respected broad-based political organisation that can speak for Cornwall'.[3] He proposed a non-inclusive role, opening membership to sympathisers within other parties and adopting an electoral strategy which would allow candidates to be jointly sponsored by MK and other parties. Meanwhile, Pedyr Prior proposed a new organisation called the 'Cornish Movement', which would also have a more flexible membership structure.[4] In the event, after considerable soul searching and debate, members reaffirmed the aims of the party and overwhelmingly supported calls to continue as a political party. At the same meeting Loveday Jenkin (see Appendix) narrowly defeated Camborne's Doreen Sjoholm to become the party's ninth Chair.

But paradoxically, just as MK was assessing whether it had any reason to celebrate its own 40th anniversary or even whether it had a future, Cornish nationalism burst onto the tabloids throughout Britain and became a *cause celebre* in metropolitan circles. Taking its cue from the widespread opposition to the poll tax, the Stannary Parliament declared the new tax to be illegal under the Stannary Laws of Cornwall which, they asserted, were still valid as confirmed by the Lord Chancellor, Elwyn Jones, as late as 1977.[5] Fred Trull of the Stannary Parliament then launched £1 shares in the 'Royal Cornish Consols United Tin Mining Cost Book Company.' It claimed that ownership of these shares made people exempt from paying the poll tax. Letters were produced for individuals to present to local district councils stating they were 'exempt from all Rates and Taxes including a Community Charge, in accordance with a Special Treaty between Cornwall and England in 1508 ...'[6]

Contrary to the news reports in the London media, this was no tax avoidance scam but a genuine attempt to force the 'first large-scale legal examination of the constitutional position of Cornwall ... as laid down in the Duchy Charters'.[7] The Department of Trade and Industry served a High Court injunction on Trull's tin company and local councils took hundreds of non-payers to court. This was despite the fact that the Department of the Environment had failed to make a ruling on the exemption claims and the whole subject remained *sub judice*, with the matter unresolved in the courts. The hoped-for investigation of the constitutional position of Cornwall was not forthcoming, though many thousands of people throughout Britain purchased the shares in an attempt to opt out of the poll tax, with some newspapers putting the figure at over one million. As postscript, the final destination of the monies collected during the episode remains shrouded in mystery.

MK re-emerges

Though the meetings of 1990 may be seen as a turning point in MK's history, the party's re-emergence as a political and electoral force was slow. In the district council elections of 1991, MK was only able to field two official candidates, neither of which was successful. The weakness of the MK label and its inability to appeal even to its own supporters at this time was demonstrated by the decision of longstanding MK district councillor Neil Plummer to seek re-election as an independent, while other leading members such as John Bolitho and Roger Holmes also preferred to stand without the party label. Similarly, in 1992 MK again chose not to contest the General Election, claiming that 'we must recognise that under the present electoral system, people will vote for the 'mainstream' candidate least offensive to them and it is difficult to persuade people, however sympathetic, to vote for a party perceived to have little chance'. Not even the news that high profile Conservative 'outsider' Sebastian Coe was to defend David Mudd's Falmouth-Camborne Constituency, could tempt the party to re-enter the fray, though a local elector famously stated of the new Tory challenger that 'he wouldn't know Tolvaddon from Tehidy ... it's the sort of thing that would make me vote for Mebyon Kernow'.[8]

The party was able to come to public attention once again on its traditional ground, however, as it continued to address issues of Cornish territoriality, calling for Cornwall's recognition as a region in its own right. MK members were able to force yet another (unsuccessful) local inquiry into calls for a Cornish Euro-seat, collecting over 3,000 signatures in about 3 months.[9] For much of this period, MK often remained the lone public voice in opposition to the formation of bodies such as the South West Enterprise Limited and the Westcountry Development Corporation, and the party quickly picked up on the demand for access to Objective One funds, the best part of a decade ahead of mainstream political parties. While a handful of other politicians, most notably Robin Teverson (Liberal Democrat MEP from 1994 to 1999) did join MK in backing calls for Cornwall to be treated as a Level 2 region in Europe to allow it to qualify for grant aid in its own right, most of the local political elite refused to follow this clear vision for Cornwall and preferred to continue their attempts to develop a 'Devonwall' agenda.

A growing number of people were therefore incensed when a 1992/ 1993 application for Objective One structural funding was nonetheless made on a Devon and Cornwall basis, in spite of the fact that Cornwall was 'bigger in area that one European nation state, seven Level One regions and thirty-two Level Two regions ... [with] a larger population than sixteen of the Level Two Regions'.[10] Although EU structural funding sought to assist regions with a GDP of less than 75 per cent of the EU average, the resulting joint Cornwall and Devon figure was well above, at 83 per cent. Cornwall with a GDP of 76 per cent was therefore denied funding while both Merseyside and the Highlands and Islands of Scotland were successful despite having higher GDP at 79 per cent of the European average.[11] For MK this was another crystal clear lesson that the 'Devonwall' project was fatally flawed and actually resulted in the institutionalisation of Cornwall's chronic economic problems rather than their alleviation.

In 1994, local government boundaries came under scrutiny, with a Local Government Review proposing the division of Cornwall into a number of unitary authorities. Faced by the possible loss of a local government body based on the historic territory of Cornwall, support was quickly gained for a cross-party pressure group 'Campaign for Cornwall', which lobbied for a 'single council for Cornwall'. In its declaration, the group stated 'we renounce any attempt to undermine the territorial integrity of Cornwall through partition into two or more administrative units',[12] its main leafleting campaign stating 'Don't let them carve-up Cornwall – we need one council with one voice for one people'. Many Cornish nationalists backed this campaign, though a number opposed the 'unitary' council for Cornwall option, which was seen as concentrating too much local influence into the hands of a County Council whose record on such issues as housing and 'Devonwall' had done little to inspire confidence about their ability to defend Cornish interests. Instead, some nationalists supported the status quo of Cornwall County Council and the six district councils, the option which eventually prevailed. Almost unanimous support was however, given to the notion that Cornwall must retain a Cornwall-wide strategic body – a fact revisited in the campaign for a Cornish Assembly in the later 1990s and onwards.

1993 saw the start of MK's third electoral phase, which continued into the new century. In that year, MK was able to field seven county council candidates with, for the first time in its history, at least one candidate in each district council area. Polling an average 17.5 per cent, the party was buoyed up and, soon after this, announced its intention to contest the 1994 Euro-election. Setting out a 'new vision for Cornwall centred on reasserting Cornwall's right to its place within a decentralised Europe of the Peoples', Party Chair Loveday Jenkin fought a strong and proactive campaign, which covered a wealth of topics from opposition to out-of-town developments and a second Tamar crossing, to calls for a Cornish

Development Agency and direct Cornish representation in Europe. The campaign nonetheless failed to garner significant support and the Cornish Stannary Parliament undermined it still further by publicly backing a Liberal candidate, when MK chose not to campaign on the agenda of the stannators. In the end, MK polled a very disappointing 3,315 votes which equated to about 2.4 per cent of the Cornish vote. Nevertheless, this electoral setback was soon followed by success at local level. Businessman Tom Tremewan won the party's first seat on Carrick District Council in a by-election at Perranporth, less than one month after the Euro-election. Ignoring considerable pressure to stand as an Independent, Tom campaigned as the 'local man in touch with his local community' and was returned in a resounding victory, polling 570 votes to the 360 of the Liberal Democrat and the 213 votes of the Tory. While this by-election victory was deemed important enough to be reported in Wales, it received virtually no mention in the Cornish media.

By the 1995 district council elections, MK was able to field nine official candidates, of which two were successful. Tom Tremewan retained his Perranporth seat with an increased vote, while MK Chair Loveday Jenkin won a seat on Kerrier District Council, polling nearly 70 per cent of votes in a three-way fight in her home parish of Crowan. At the same time, Bude's John Bolitho, once again standing on an MK ticket, missed out on election by only 45 votes. Parish and town councillors were also elected from Liskeard in the east to Gwennap in the west. MK gained a further district councillor in November, this time due to a defection. Expelled from the Labour Party following disputes over committee chairmanships, Penwith councillor Ruth Lewarne, who represented Penzance West, sat for a number of months as an 'Independent Left' councillor, before crossing the floor to join MK which she described as the only 'party determined to speak for Cornwall'.[13] Encouraged by this progress at local level, MK's 1995 Conference took the decision to fight a majority of Cornish seats at the next General Election, to give local people 'the opportunity to vote for a principled party, fighting on a distinctly Cornish platform'.[14]

MK's renewed electoral interventions in the mid 1990s came at a time when Cornwall's councils had become more party-politicised. Cornwall County Council, Carrick District Council and Restormel Borough Council had all at some stage come under Liberal Democrat control. Taking this development into account, MK developed a lobbying strategy to work in tandem with its elections. The lobbying, often followed by recorded votes in the council chamber, was designed both to pressure and inform representatives of the London parties, to highlight to the wider public who were both sympathisers and implacable opponents. Spearheaded by Colin Lawry and press officer Dick Cole (see

Appendix), the strategy was relatively successful in causing considerable political embarrassment to Cornwall's Liberal Democrats, driving
policy wedges between its MPs and councillors. For example, a survey
of the views of MPs and some leading councillors on the establishment
of a Cornish Assembly was published in May 1995 which found considerable support for the concept from MPs, parliamentary candidates
and leading councillors from all left-leaning political parties. This was
followed by MK's allies raising the issue at Westminster. Cynog Dafis
and Dafydd Wigley of Plaid Cymru and Margaret Ewing of the SNP put
down an Early Day Motion calling for a Cornish Assembly, which was
then backed by Cornwall's two Liberal Democrat MPs, Matthew Taylor
and Paul Tyler. However, a subsequent motion to Cornwall County
Council in December was defeated, as Liberal Democrat councillors
effectively voted against their own MPs, putting forward what was
described as a 'wrecking amendment … neither opposed to or in favour
of a Cornish Assembly'.[15]

Similarly, MK was to the forefront of the campaign for a Cornish Development Agency (CDA), a campaign that it had itself first launched in
the 1960s. A series of unsuccessful motions were presented to Cornwall
County Council in 1995 and 1996; MK ridiculed the decision of two
committees not to support the campaign but finally succeeded in encouraging the Council to back a CDA early in the election year of 1997 with
near unanimity. Yet again it was noticeable both how election years focused attention on Cornish issues and also how such resolutions could
be passed as matters of principle but were then rarely acted on. Such
resolutions did little, if anything, in practice to stem the rush to merge
Cornish institutions with Devon-based administrative bodies.

1997 and the election of a Labour Government

By 1997, Cornwall's serious social and economic problems were gradually becoming more widely known. After 18 years of Conservative rule,
Cornwall's GDP had plummeted to less than 75 per cent of the EU
average, male wages were the lowest in Britain at just 77 per cent of the
average, low-level deprivation was widespread with the relative poverty of many Cornish households showing up in statistics relating to
chronic ill health.[16] Even better-off incomers, research showed, often
found themselves drifting down to the local income level rather than
being dynamic poles of wealth creation.[17] Although Cornwall's 'holiday image' had helped to prevent these chronic social problems from

becoming major political issues, it was noticeable that the late 1980s and early 90s had shown a larger than average swing away from Conservatism in Cornwall.

For Mebyon Kernow all three main political parties were equally 'bland and irrelevant' in their response to these socio-economic problems, just offering 'different versions of Tory policies'. The party fought four of Cornwall's five parliamentary constituencies in the May 1997 General Election. Its campaign was based around a comprehensive 18,000 word manifesto – *Cornwall 2000 – The Way Ahead* – which had been adopted at the preceding party conference. Founded on four cornerstones, the manifesto was described as 'Cornish, Green, Left-of-Centre and Decentralist'. Three of the candidates had been selected in the spring of 1996, namely Ruth Lewarne (Falmouth-Camborne), John Bolitho (North Cornwall) and Liskeard's Paul Dunbar (South-East Cornwall). Davyth Hicks, a post-graduate student at Edinburgh University, was later chosen to contest Truro and St. Austell, while activists in St. Ives decided not to contest that constituency, publicly giving their support to former MK member Andrew George, who was making his second attempt to win the seat for the Liberal Democrats.

MK was able to raise its game for the 1997 elections and the Cornwall County Council poll, which took place on the same day. In the period leading up to and including election day over 300,000 leaflets were distributed. In spite of this, there was to be no historic breakthrough. With the Conservatives in complete disarray following personal and financial scandals, infighting over Europe, the collapse of the ERM on Black Wednesday and unpopular policies such as VAT on domestic fuel, voters chose to swing in their thousands to the non-Tory alternative most likely to eject John Major's government. MK's parliamentary votes were poor, with the four candidates polling an aggregate of only 1,906, not many more than had been won in each of the two western seats in 1979. But the County Council results were considerably better. MK's thirteen candidates, scattered from Penzance to Bude and Callington, polled an average of over 500 votes, while Colin Lawry retained his Newlyn seat with 2,606 votes against his Tory opponent's 1,088. The elections were, moreover, a signal that Mebyon Kernow had returned as a party with the determination and ability to contest elections at all levels, across the length and breadth of Cornwall.

Labour's landslide victory of 1997 was initially met with enthusiasm in Cornwall. The Liberal Democrats won four of Cornwall's five seats while Candy Atherton had captured Falmouth-Camborne for Labour, and many proudly proclaimed Cornwall a 'Tory-free Zone' just like Wales and Scotland. Andrew George won St. Ives and, beginning his political career with a speech that included a few words of Cornish, soon effectively established himself as a pro-Cornish MP. Supporting most campaigns dear to the hearts of Cornish nationalists, he has also sought to distance himself from the more ethnic nationalist fringe. His position resembles the anti-metropolitan agenda of his 1960s Liberal forebears, Bessell and Pardoe, and in addition he plays the Cornish card in a manner reminiscent of the highly regarded MP of the 1970s and 1980s David Penhaligon. Andrew George's position on Cornish matters has been more consistent, and he has offered strong support to devolution campaigns. At the same time George's powerbase has made the St. Ives constituency a more difficult electoral area for MK. The price of supporting a 'nationalist' MP has thus been to restrict the development of a 'nationalist' organisation in Penwith, in the past one of MK's more promising electoral areas.

In the meantime, many activists took a rest from the day to day grind of the political world to commemorate the 500th anniversary of the Cornish uprising of 1497. Organised by Keskerdh Kernow 500, some 50 individuals retraced the steps of the rebels, Michael Joseph An Gof and Thomas Flamank, from St. Keverne to Blackheath. Thousands turned out to take part in the start of the march, again when it crossed the Tamar into England at Launceston's Polson Bridge and at its end in London, while many hundreds of others joined the march along the way for various distances. Though deliberately portrayed by the organisers as a cultural event and educational experience, the march graphically demonstrated the strength of feeling about Cornish identity and very few doubted the political overtones of the 1997 marchers. Newspapers like the *Western Morning News* noted how it was 'about much more than simply remembering and revelling in the past' adding that Cornwall still suffered 'injustices and hardships compared to other parts of Britain'.[18] The Keskerdh Kernow celebrations showed the extent to which there was now a growing desire by Cornish people to express and celebrate their own identity, as they did during the Cornish rugby successes of 1989, 1991 and 1992 when thousands of fans took the 'Cornish cause into the capital of foreign England'.[19] The popular use of symbols such as the Cornish flag and the black and gold rugby colours as well as the Cornish tartan was mushrooming and even extended to MK's political opponents who began to use these symbols for their own political advantage.

The marchers themselves, upon reaching Blackheath, set out a series of political demands, including a Cornish Development Agency, Cornish Euro-seat, a university campus in Cornwall and the teaching of Cornish history, culture and language in schools. It was also during the Keskerdh Kernow march that a further small group of disaffected nationalists formed the An Gof National Party, hoping to capitalise on the positive publicity of the commemorative march. It made a number of claims about the right of Cornish people to break the law if it was needed but, like most of the sporadic right-wing Cornish organisations that had appeared since the Greenshirts of the late 1970s, rapidly disappeared from view.

The optimism of the marchers and Cornwall as a whole in the summer of 1997 was shortlived. While activists in the Cornish movement looked to the forthcoming devolution referenda in Wales and Scotland as a sign of better things to come, all hopes for the greater recognition of Cornwall were crushed as central government proceeded to impose a development agency that stretched from the Isles of Scilly to Swindon. MK condemned this body as undemocratic and a 'final insidious move to undermine Cornwall, its people and their aspirations for the future'.[20] But MK found itself effectively sidelined as the pre-election consensus in favour of a Cornish Development Agency collapsed, with councillors unwilling to oppose proposals from the new government. The Chief Executive of Cornwall County Council put forward a recommendation to the council advising them to support the government proposals. This was roundly condemned throughout Cornwall, not least by the Liberal Democrat MP Matthew Taylor who railed that 'the Chief Executive can make what recommendations he likes, but I don't think that is going to change the views of councillors that the best way ahead is for Cornwall to have its own development agency'.[21] But Matthew Taylor's view of Liberal Democrat unity was misplaced. All but two of their councillors backtracked from their earlier position, along with all the Conservative and Labour members. At the same time, yet another local inquiry to assess Cornish demands for a Euro-seat rejected the claim to a separate Euro-constituency. This time, the inquiry was held at a safe distance from Cornwall in Taunton.

At about the same time the Cornish economy seemed to go into freefall, with over 1400 job losses announced in the second half of 1997. By August, the news broke that Cornwall's last working tin mine – South Crofty – was to close with the loss of over 270 jobs. Cornish nationalists held an immediate demonstration at the gates of the mine, with each person taking a yellow flower from a wreath which the protesters claimed did not commemorate the death of the mine but was a symbol of its fight for the future. This was soon followed by the closure of Abru Aluminium at Launceston, Finns Shoes at Penzance, the St. Ivel Creamery at St. Erth as well as considerable downsizing in a number of traditionally strong Cornish companies such as English China Clays, Compair Holman and Maxam. Such was the economic downturn that one local newspaper felt Cornwall faced the 'humiliating prospect of becoming a giant theme park with a cast of forelock tugging yokels taking crumbs from the tourists' tables'.[22]

South Crofty, the Millennium Convention and Cornish Solidarity

The prospects of a constitutional convention or forum for Cornwall had been a regular topic of internal debate within MK from as early as 1992, but came to the fore at the same time as the closure of South Crofty. Elected as Party Chairman in October 1997, Dick Cole used his acceptance speech at the Party Conference to focus on Labour's unwillingness to recognise Cornwall as a political entity. He addressed what would be needed to win an assembly for Cornwall, calling for the setting up of a cross-party constitutional convention. The aim was to bring together supporters of devolution from all political parties. Following the tacit approval of party members, the newly-elected MP for St. Ives Andrew George was approached and a series of meetings took place in 1997–1998 to push the idea forward. These brought together businessmen and women, former miners, academics and cultural activists. Termed the 'Cornish Millennium Convention', the group produced a document entitled *Into the Millennium or into Oblivion?*, which claimed it was a 'bold and visionary plan to lead Cornwall forward into the next millennium'. The decision was taken to launch the Convention on 8th March 1998, deliberately coinciding with the protests at the closure of South Crofty, in an attempt to maximise publicity. In fact the exact opposite happened, with the news media largely ignoring the event and choosing instead to concentrate on the birth of the pressure group Cornish Solidarity.

Anger about the closure of South Crofty had already been the catalyst for an impromptu protest drawing attention to Cornwall's economic plight. Frustration boiled over into action as campaigners from a wide range of Cornish organisations came together spontaneously to block the A30 trunk road out of Cornwall with a slow-moving convoy in February 1998. Born of this event, Cornish Solidarity set about campaigning on a platform which overlapped in many respects with that of MK. They set out the by now familiar nationalist demands of Objective One status for Cornwall, a Cornish Development Agency, Cornwall's own MEP, a Cornish University, democratic control over a Cornish health service and support for traditional industries and culture.[23] The group also came to support the fight for a Cornish Assembly. Capitalising on a media desperate for event-driven stories, Solidarity organised a series of demonstrations which included the 'penny protest' at the Tamar Bridge, linking Cornwall to England, when tolls were paid in copper. 'We shall pay our tolls in pennies because that's all we've got left to pay with in Cornwall' said Greg Woods, the Chairman of the Group. Cornish Solidarity's last major event was 'Operation Trelawny' in July 1998 when over 1,000 people with banners marched on the Tamar Bridge, symbolically blocking the 'Bridge Too Far'.[24] In contrast, the Millennium Convention had proved a dismal failure. The launch at the Hall for Cornwall had been well attended but poorly reported, with the end product being bland compared to the direct action of Cornish Solidarity.

Objective One

The main campaigning plank of the Solidarity movement was the continuing demand for Objective One funding for Cornwall. The first task in the struggle to obtain Objective One funding had been to uncouple Cornwall and Devon, the existing European Level Two region and the area eligible for Objective One grant aid. In 1996 various Cornish organisations had orchestrated a concerted Cornwall-wide campaign to support the separation of Cornwall and Devon. In that year, over 20 per cent of all representations to an Office of National Statistics (ONS) UK-wide consultation came from Cornwall, with the majority penned by MK members and associated cultural and political groups. The ONS backed Cornish calls for separation, making the recommendation that Cornwall should indeed stand alone as a Level 2 European region. In 1998 Eurostat, the European Commission's statistical service, supported the redrawing of the European regional map, recognising Cornwall's 'distinct cultural and historical factors reflecting a Celtic background'.[25]

By this time, Cornwall's GDP had slipped to just 69 per cent of the EU average and the political establishment in both Cornwall and London finally woke up to the possibility of Objective One funding. After years of dismissing the possibility of such funding as 'unrealistic', the first few months of 1998 saw the unedifying and incredible spectacle of various previously staunch defenders of 'Devonwall' desperately waving the Cornish flag and climbing onto the structural funds bandwagon. While they were new converts to the cause of Objective 1 funding, they nonetheless refused to learn its lesson – that the 'Devonwall' politics of the 1980s and 1990s had failed. For the years of institutional merger that had preceded it directly contradicted structural funding based on Cornwall's status as a European region. In contrast, establishment support for Objective 1 was a way of continuing business as usual. For the 'Devonwall' status quo was now being shaken to its roots as the Labour Government pushed on with its own regionalisation project based on Cornwall and the six counties of South West England. Supporting Objective One and playing a key role in the partnership that would control the funding process was the only way, the former enthusiasts of 'Devonwall' could hold on to their local power base. At the same time they had the option of scrabbling for a place at the table of the peak 'south west' institutions. In no time at all, the Objective 1 campaign had been reduced to a simplistic slogan with structural funding viewed as the answer to all problems, just as massive population growth had been the solution in the 1970s or 'Devonwall' in the 1980s. The opportunity, to build on Cornwall's European regional status to demand a wholesale reversal of the institutional drift to 'south west' regionalisation, was again thrown away.

Cornwall's official status as an Objective One region was announced in March 1999. But again there was a failure to match this with the institutions required to guarantee Cornish control of the outcome. Calls for a Cornish Assembly, reformed local government and new Cornish private sector institutions were ignored. For many, victory was transformed into defeat. MK quickly pointed out the inconsistency of 'arguing that Cornwall should be a unit in Europe, while at the same time it is not allowed any form of regional status within Britain'[26] but there was no will in government to address the continuing vacuum at the centre of Cornish governance. Although nationalists could celebrate that the 'Devonwall' project was now dead in the water, increasing political power was, however, being divested into the hands of the new Government Office of the South West, together with the Regional Development Agency and the South West 'Regional Assembly'; the latter two unelected and unaccountable bodies and all based outside Cornwall.

New battles ... old battles

Within the new political climate, Mebyon Kernow continued to develop and define its political philosophy as progressive, inclusive and outward-looking. Openly campaigning for all the people of Cornwall, the party relaunched itself as 'Mebyon Kernow – the Party for Cornwall' in 1999. A clear attempt to distance itself from its less politically correct 'Sons of Cornwall' label, this proposal was put to the party membership through a postal ballot and won the support of over 95 per cent of members. Many of the political campaigns fought by MK after 1997 revisited the battles of the previous 45 years. The issues were often the same – only the context and detail were different. Recognition of Cornwall's distinct needs and aspirations formed a central plank of many campaigns as did the party's opposition to centralisation and the loss of services. Added to these traditional concerns Mebyon Kernow also spoke out against Third World Debt, the Arms Trade and in 2001 was the only political group in Cornwall to condemn the US/UK bombing of Afghanistan. With the shift of 'New Labour' to the right, the contradictory stances adopted by Liberal Democrat MPs in Westminster and the party's councillors in Cornwall, and the weakness of the Greens, MK was often the most radical voice in Cornish politics after 1997.

As far as Cornwall's nationalists were concerned it soon became apparent that, in many respects, New Labour was no different from the Tories. A Learning and Skills Council was created for Cornwall and Devon despite widespread opposition. This replaced the Training and Enterprise Council that had been slipped through at the height of the 'Devonwall' campaign in 1986. The opportunity to rationalise the boundaries of the over-large Devon and Cornwall TEC was not grasped, partly through the opposition of the Labour Party in Plymouth. Worse news was to come. An earlier success, Cornwall's Office in Brussels, was abolished in 2000 to be replaced by a South West Office. As a result, Cornwall lost its distinct presence at the heart of the EU. This was a barely credible decision in the light of Cornwall's new status as a European region. Continuing these short-sighted policies, control of Cornwall's Probation Service was lost while, in opposition to the wishes of its own workforce, the National Trust regions of Cornwall and Devon were merged in March 2002. This was immediately followed by the merger of the Cornwall and Isles of Scilly Health Authority with that of Devon in April 2002, in spite of a well-supported MK campaign of opposition. By 2002 it appeared that there was no Cornish-based institution left to merge with Devon.

Cornish cultural activists fared somewhat better in their fight for recognition from Westminster. As early as 1995, the UK and 21 other member states of the Council of Europe had signed a Framework Convention for the Protection of National Minorities, aimed at combating discrimination while promoting the culture and identity of minority groups. The new Government's compliance report finally appeared in 1999. It openly recognised the need to give protection to the heritage of the Welsh, Scottish and Irish, but at the same time argued that the Cornish did not constitute a national minority. A wide array of campaigners came together to contest this injustice. Independent councillor Bert Biscoe assembled a steering group which organized the publication of a report, which challenged this lack of recognition.[27] Addressed to the relevant Advisory Committee of the Council of Ministers, it demanded a detailed study of the Cornish situation in relation to the Framework Convention. In a similar move, the UK Government also ratified the Charter for the Protection of Regional and Minority Languages but then, at first, argued that Cornish was not covered – while at the same time making the very political decision to ensure that the 'dialect' of Ulster Scots was. Such was the government confusion over the Cornish Language at this time that it couldn't even decide which department was responsible for language policy. Representations passed between the Welsh Office and the

Home Office, landing up at one stage at the Foreign Office – an irony not lost on Cornish nationalists and the Labour MP Paul Flynn – before ending up with the Government Office of the South-West. But progress was to be made. The Government Office of the South West sponsored a report by Professor Ken MacKinnon and ongoing pressure over a two year period culminated in an official 'leak' in July 2002 that the Minister responsible was close to announcing the UK's inclusion of Cornish at the Part II level of the Charter, giving the language an official status that will help safeguard moves to protect and promote it. Prior to this, 1999 had already seen one small victory. The existence of the Cornish as a distinct ethnic group was recognized by the Office of National Statistics for the first time, albeit by civil servants who bypassed central government ministers. The ONS allocated a local code to the Cornish relating to the 'ethnic identity' question in the 2001 census, which allowed people to tick the 'Other' box and write in 'Cornish'. Unfortunately, the usefulness of the question for any monitoring of the employment or housing conditions of the ethnic groups of Cornwall was undermined by the South West Regional Development Agency. This body refused to supply any funding to market the question so that people in Cornwall might be convinced of its importance.

While government refusal to recognize the Cornish as a distinct group was viewed by nationalists as bad enough in its own right, this had come on top of the imposition of an 'English' national curriculum in schools and the impact of other anglicizing bodies such as English Heritage and the South West RDA. Many in the wider movement looked outside the normal political process to have their say. There was an intensification of the clandestine campaign of physical damage to English Heritage and English rose tourism signs which had spluttered on since the mid-1980s. The signs of government quangos such as English Partnerships and the South West of England Regional Development Agency also became major targets and such was the widespread nature of the campaign, that Cornwall County Council removed all English roses from its tourist signs during the latter half of 2001. At the same time, it launched a consultation on the adoption of a distinctly 'Cornish symbol' to replace it. Meanwhile, in an echo of the proposed CATER campaign of the mid-1980s, the Cornish Stannary Parliament had launched 'Operation Chough', its own systematic and highly publicized 'confiscation' of English Heritage signs from ancient monuments in Cornwall. From the courtyard houses at Chysauster in the west to Tintagel Castle on the north coast, signs were removed between January and November 2000 by three members of the Parliament, who also displayed photographs of the action on the group's website, the signs being held in safe custody as 'evidence of English cultural aggression in Cornwall'. The 'Stannary Three' were eventually arrested near Pendennis Castle in November 2000. In the subsequent courtcase, the Crown offered no evidence for prosecution and the three Cornishmen agreed to be bound over to keep the peace while making a token payment towards the damage caused, claiming this end result was a public admission that 'English Heritage has never had cultural legitimacy in Cornwall'.[28]

The growth in electioneering

Proportional representation arrived in Cornwall in 1998, when it was announced that the 1999 elections to the European Parliament would use multi-member constituencies. But Cornwall was lost within a huge South West constituency which, together with a £5000 deposit, debarred MK from fighting the election. The new constituency also removed sympathetic local Liberal Democrat Robin Teverson, who lost his seat, while his less supportive colleague Graham Watson retained his. Yet, in spite of being forced out of the Euro-elections, MK entered its most active period of electioneering at local level, putting forward nearly 60 candidates in elections to principal authorities between 1999 and 2001. Twenty-four candidates contested the district council elections of May 1999 and three were successful. Loveday Jenkin retained her seat on Kerrier District Council unopposed, John Bolitho took Bude in North Cornwall with one of the highest personal votes in Cornwall while Party Leader Dick Cole won MK's first seat on Restormel Borough Council. MK members also won a record number of seats on town and parish councils, including long-serving councillors such as Roger Holmes and Graham Sandercock at Liskeard as well as newcomer Alan Sanders at Camborne. Alan himself was subsequently joined by Stuart Cullimore and Helene Ranson, who won by-elections to the same council in 2000 and 2002 respectively.

In 2001, MK fought three seats in the June General Election – increasing the MK vote to two-and-a-half times that of 1997. Conan Jenkin and Ken George achieved the party's best-ever results in Truro and St. Austell and South-East Cornwall respectively, polling 1137 and 1209 (both 2.3 per cent). Hilda Wasley meanwhile fought a campaign of great energy and enterprise in the so-called 'three way marginal' of Falmouth-Camborne and won 853 votes (1.8 per cent). Nevertheless, the mean MK vote in 2001 remained below the average of 1979 and, unlike then, was lower than all Plaid Cymru and SNP candidates in the same election. On the other hand, MK out-performed the Breton autonomist party, the UDB, whose 33 candidates in the French Legislative elections of 2002 polled between 0.6 per cent and 2.2 per cent.

The Cornwall County Council elections of 2001 took place on the same day as the General Election. This political environment meant that MK candidates at both levels found it very difficult to gain any coverage from either the local or London TV and radio media. Indeed, serious coverage of MK's views was deemed less newsworthy than media spectacles like Ann Widdecombe of the Tories visiting Penzance and pretending to eat a pasty in Market Jew Street. BBC Radio Cornwall meanwhile hosted live constituency debates, but the MK parliamentary candidates were only allowed one third of the time allocated to the candidates of the main London-based parties.[29] In spite of this, MK polled nearly 5 per cent of those votes cast in the council elections for political parties, although standing in just over a quarter of the 79 seats. MK candidates managed an average of 405 votes compared with 215 for the continuing Liberal Party, 694 for Labour, 897 for the Tories and 1241 for the Liberal Democrats.

Table 1: MK candidates at Local Elections

1974–77	1978–81	1982–85	1986–89	1990–93	1994–97	1998–01
13	35	21	9	11	26	59

Table 2: CNP candidates at Local Elections

1974–77	1978–81	1982–85	1986–89	1990–93	1994–97	1998–01
0	5	7	0	0	0	0

This third wave of electioneering for MK, although not attaining the long-awaited breakthrough at parliamentary level, served to consolidate the party's presence at local government level. In the period 1998–2001 MK contested 63 per cent more seats than in its previous peak of activity twenty years earlier. Moreover, the spread of candidates in this latter period was noticeably more dispersed geographically, introducing MK to a growing number of Cornish voters. Until then, a feature of MK's electioneering activity had been a geographical concentration of candidates, with a clustering in Kerrier District in the 1974–81 period giving way to Penwith over 1978–85. In the most recent phase, candidates have stood in all Cornish districts although being thicker on the ground in mid-Cornwall, in a belt of wards from Camborne in the west through Truro to the St. Austell district in the east. As well as demonstrating a recent growth in the number of MK candidates, this shifting pattern of activity has partly reflected the location of its core activists over the years, from Camborne-Redruth in the 1970s to Penwith in the early 1980s to mid-Cornwall in the late 1990s/early 2000s.

Before the late 1990s there had been some suggestion of a west-east gradient in MK's voting support. Other factors being equal the party appeared to poll higher in the west than in the east, although this pattern has been less clear cut in recent years (see the 1997 and 2001 General Elections, for example). Comparative analysis of MK's more recent election performances is made very difficult by a number of factors. The first is the shifting geography noted above, while the second is the changing context of local politics in Cornwall.

Table 3: Mean MK vote (%) in single seat contests at local elections (no. of contests)

	1974–77	1978–81	1982–85	1986–89	1990–93	1994–97	1998–01
All contests	22.3 (9)	18.5 (18)	25.4 (16)	30.0 (7)	24.5 (10)	16.9 (17)	13.9 (38)
Contests with at least three other candidates	none	7.9 (4)	16.5 (7)	8.0 (1)	7.0 (3)	8.4 (10)	9.7 (21)

As shown above in Table 3, MK is increasingly likely to face three or more candidates as the other parties themselves contest a higher proportion of seats. Of the twenty-one contests in the 2001 County Council elections, fifteen featured between four and six candidates. In these well contested fights, MK's average poll was 10.3 per cent, a noticeable increase from 8.1 per cent in comparable wards in 1993 and 7.6 per cent in 1997. But such heavily contested elections were much less common before 1994 and this makes the electoral task of MK in turn that much more difficult. Nevertheless, overall the MK vote seems to have held up in the 8–10 per cent area in four-candidate contests. This proportion is very similar to that obtained by the German Green Party in Federal and Regional elections.

Limited analysis also showed that in the 1970s and early 1980s the MK vote was positively correlated with the proportion of council house tenants, probably as these wards contained the highest numbers of Cornish born voters.[30] No similar study has been carried out on voting patterns in the most recent phase of MK electioneering, although there have been some suggestions that MK now attracts a higher proportion of its votes from 'progressive incomers' and the middle classes.[31] If true, this development may bode well for the party in winning support from the modern-day, more diverse, Cornish population.

50,000 for Cornish Assembly

Meanwhile, the new millennium provided evidence that MK's electoral support was only the tip of a much larger iceberg for support for some kind of devolution. On St. Piran's Day (5th March) 2000, MK had launched a declaration campaign that was to grab the imagination of the people of Cornwall. Clearly stating that 'Cornwall is a nation with its own identity, culture, traditions and history' the declaration called for a 'Cornish Assembly that could set the right democratic priorities for Cornwall and provide a stronger voice for our communities in Britain, in Europe and throughout the wider world'. This campaign soon took to the streets and gathered a momentum all of its own. Under the guidance of Paddy McDonough, teams of petitioners made up of individuals from MK and from other organisations spent time almost each and every weekend signing up thousands of supporters from St. Just to Millbrook. The symbolic 20,000th signature belonged to Dean Shipton, the captain of the 1999 championship winning Cornish rugby team and, by the summer of 2001, a total of 50,000 signatures had been collected in the space of fifteen months. Equivalent to 10 per cent of the Cornish electorate, campaigners presented a list of the declaration's supporters on a CD-ROM to 10 Downing St. and demanded Tony Blair bring forward the necessary legislation and referendum. Though at first an MK initiative, the declarations became much more than that. Support came from across the political spectrum, including four of Cornwall's five MPs and over 130 councillors from all parties. Support from outside Cornwall was also strong including MPs, MEPs and AMs from Plaid Cymru, SNP MSPs and even several members of the Irish Dail, most notably Eamon O Cuiv, the then Minister of State at the Department of Agriculture and the grandson of Eamon De Valera.

Running in tandem with the declaration campaign was the launch and growth of the Cornish Constitutional Convention. Frustrated by the failure of the Millennium Convention and the growing strength of regionalism in England, MK Leader Dick Cole, Independent councillor Bert Biscoe and Stephen Horscroft came together to launch a Constitutional Convention for Cornwall. This followed the 'Whose Regions?' Conference at Launceston, organised by MK and the English devolution pressure group Devolve, at which rumours of the impending launch of a South West Constitutional Convention began to circulate. The inaugural meeting took place at County Hall in Truro on July 7th 2000. Uniting around a statement which declared that the people of Cornwall 'will be best served in their future governance by a Cornish regional assembly', there was widespread support from throughout Cornwall. The launch was addressed by a range of speakers including Tory parliamentary candidate Nick Serpell and Andrew George MP. There was some opposition from within the wider Cornish movement however, with the Stannary Parliament arguing vigorously that the approach of the Convention compromised the existing 'legitimacy' of Cornwall's Stannary rights, caricaturing the campaign as English regionalism rather than Cornish nationalism.

Central government had nonetheless already set up unelected Regional Assemblies (the former Regional Chambers) throughout 'England', and in 2001 awarded each £500,000 to oversee the activities of Regional Development Agencies. The Cornish Constitutional Convention set about persuading central government that it had to look outside its standard planning regions if it was going to deliver devolution successfully. The Convention twice met with government minsters and forged solid working relationships with other constitutional conventions, while setting out its plans for a Cornish Assembly in March 2002 with the publication of *Devolution for One and All*, which called for the setting up of a Cornish Assembly with powers equal to those of the Welsh Assembly. The Convention's research team also tried to show that under a Cornish Assembly local communities would be much better off. One key finding showed that Cornwall was losing £59 million per year as a result of administrative activities being based outside Cornwall. At the same time, funding Cornwall through the Barnett Formula as in Wales and Scotland would have generated an extra £101 million per annum for the Cornish economy.[32] Such work was reinforced by a report on the Cornish economy promoted by *Business Age* magazine, which stated bluntly that London was 'raping Cornwall financially'. Claiming that Cornish communities put a great deal more into the Exchequer's pot than they ever get back, the article noted that: 'Out of a tiny gross domestic product of 3.6 billion pounds, the Government takes over 1.95 billion in taxes, and puts back into Cornwall less than 1.62 billion, a gap of over £300 million'.[33] At the same time, the report investigated the impact of people in Cornwall paying an enormous amount of their weekly incomes to insurance companies, banks and building societies for mortgages and various loans – the financial benefit of which does not stay in Cornwall.

Building on 50 years of political activity calling for self government for Cornwall, the Convention, alongside MK and a range of other bodies, had orchestrated the most powerful campaign for a new democratic settlement from anywhere in the UK. The Government's White Paper setting out their proposals for regional government was therefore eagerly awaited. John Prescott finally outlined his vision of regional government for England in the House of Commons in May 2002. Entitled '*Your Region, Your Choice; Revitalising the English Regions*', the White Paper proposed directly elected, regional assemblies for the Government's standard planning regions. Stretching to 111 pages, the document failed to make a single mention of the case for devolution to Cornwall and studiously ignored the fact that over 50,000 people had signed individual declaration forms calling for a Cornish Assembly. Writing in the preface, Tony Blair claimed the White Paper was about choice, stating 'where there is public support' for regional government, people would be allowed a referendum on the issue.[34] But for Cornwall, there was apparently no choice. John Prescott presented just one option – a 25–35 seat assembly for the 'South West,' with extremely limited powers, that lumped Cornwall in with Devon, Somerset, Dorset, Gloucestershire, Wiltshire and Bristol.

There were a range of immediate responses from the wider Cornish movement. Andrew George MP attacked the Government's 'control freak' tendencies and called for devolution to 'regions which actually exist, rather than synthetic places created by them'.[35] Bert Biscoe, Chairman of the Cornish Constitutional Convention, described the White Paper as the 'opening pitch in the game' adding 'Prescott … will be hearing from us'.[36] MK's message meanwhile was blunt and uncompromising. The party declared that the proposals made a 'mockery' of the democratic aspirations of the people of Cornwall while new MK Councillor Phil Rendle, who had one week earlier retained Colin Lawry's seat on Penwith Council, declared 'the future of Cornwall, perhaps its very existence is at stake'.[37] There was a near-unanimous call from leaders of the campaign for activists not to be downhearted, but to redouble and intensify their efforts to win a Cornish Assembly. The proposals also met with little enthusiasm in the wider Cornish community. The Government's unwillingness to invite debate on boundaries, the very limiting range of political powers and the fact that Cornwall would elect only two assembly members were among the more contentious issues which became staples of political debate through the spring and summer of 2002. Cornwall County Council, four of Cornwall's six district councils and numerous town and parish councils backed the campaign for a Cornish Assembly and/or a referendum, while the Convention and associated Cornish groups sponsored successful postcard and letter writing campaigns. In spite of this, the Government has, thus far, shown little wish to move away from its White Paper proposals, with Ministers continuing to emphasise they 'do not propose to depart from the existing boundaries used by the Government Offices'.[38]

So, 50 years after MK launched itself in Redruth's Oates Temperance Hotel, the campaign for greater Cornish self-government found itself at an important juncture. Perhaps for the first time, there was clear, quantifiable and growing evidence of support in Cornwall for a devolution settlement. But at the same time, the Government in Westminster displayed familiar signs of intransigence and an unwillingness to redraft its proposals to meet demands from the far west.

Notes

1. *Western Morning News*, April 20 1990.
2. *Western Morning News*, April 23 1990.
3. Bernard Deacon (1990), *MK: A Political Movement for the 1990s*, included in MK mailing, 28 July 1990.
4. Pedyr Prior (1990), *Mebyon Kernow – Proposals for the Future*, included in MK mailing, 28 July 1990.
5. *Kernow*, 8 (February/March 1990), p. 14.
6. The stannators claimed that the 1508 'Treaty had been Ratified by the Cornish Stannary Parliament and the United Kingdom Parliament [and was] Valid to this present day'. The reference for the relevant documentation was given as CR23 HenVII, Pt 11, mm 29–31, dated 12th July, 1508.
7. *Kernow*, 8 (April/May 1990), p. 2.
8. Quote in *West Briton*, reproduced in *Free Cornwall* 9 (October 1989) p. 2.
9. *Western Morning News*, 25 November 1993.
10. MK press release, 5 February 1993.
11. Philip Payton (1992), *The Making of Modern Cornwall*, Redruth, p. 234.
12. *Cornish World*, 1 (June 1994).
13. MK press release, 27 November 1995.
14. *West Briton*, 9 November 1995.
15. *Western Morning News*, 28 December 1995.
16. Bernard Deacon (1999), *The Cornish and the Council of Europe Framework Convention for the Protection of National Minorities*, Truro, pp. 19–20.
17. Malcolm Williams, Brain Cheal, Peter Mitchell and Lyn Bryant (1995) *Movers and Stayers: Population and Social Change in Cornwall 1971–1991*, Plymouth.
18. *Western Morning News*, 25 June 1997.
19. Cited in Payton (1993), *Cornwall Since the War*, Exeter, p. 244.
20. *Cornish Guardian*, 6 August 1998.
21. *Western Morning News*, 5 July, 1997.
22. *Cornishman*, 12 February 1998.
23. *Western Morning News*, 5 March 1998.
24. *West Briton*, 30 July 1998.
25. Office of National Statistics press release, 29 June 1998.
26. *West Briton*, 4 June 1998.
27. Bernard Deacon (1999), *The Cornish and the Council of Europe*.
28. *Western Morning News*, 19 January 2002.
29. This was a slight improvement from the 1997 General Election when MK candidates were not allowed to participate in the debates.
30. Bernard Deacon (1983), 'The electoral impact of Cornish Nationalism', in Cathal O'Luain, *For a Celtic Future: A tribute to Alan Heusaff*, Dublin, pp. 243–252.
31. Communication to the authors from Malcolm Williams.
32. Cornish Constitutional Convention research papers on *Economic Development Powers* (July 2001) and the *Barnett Formula* (August 2001). These were compiled by Andrew Climo Thompson.

33. Kevin Cahill (2001), 'The Killing of Cornwall', *Business Age* Magazine. Re-printed in *Cornish Nation* 23 (Autumn 2001), pp. 4–5.
34. Department of Transport, Local Government and the Regions (2002), *Your Region, Your Choice. Revitalising the English Regions*, London.
35. Liberal Democrat press release, 14 May 2002.
36. *Western Morning News*, 1 May 2002.
37. *Cornish Nation* 26 (Summer 2002), p. 4.
38. Government Minister Nick Raynsford MP in Hansard, 10 Jun 2002, Column 1022W.

VIII

CULTURE AND POLITICS: ASSESSING CORNISH NATIONALISM

What have been the achievements and disappointments of 50 years of political nationalism in Cornwall? What does history tell us and what opportunities might the future hold for Cornish nationalism and for MK?

English politics and Celtic culture

In 1965, just before MK's first surge of growth, founder-members Richard and Ann Jenkin argued that the emergence of MK had been 'one of the most promising signs that Cornwall will continue to exist as a Celtic country and not decline into merely an administrative division of England'.[1] In fact, perhaps unexpectedly, both these developments have occurred. Far from being opposites they have proved to be quite compatible. Since the 1960s there has been an unmistakeable enrichment and intensification of the Cornish sense of 'Celtic' identity. However, at the same time, Cornwall has indeed 'declined' into a state of what should more accurately be described as being part of an administrative division of England, rather then even being an administrative division of England in its own right.

From a nationalist perspective ultimately the biggest failure of half a century of organised nationalism must be the inability to achieve any measure of devolution. This is in stark contrast to Scotland and Wales, where Plaid Cymru and the SNP are now the official opposition within devolved assemblies. In Cornwall the opposite has occurred. During the lifetime of MK, and especially since the 1960s, the processes of 'Devonwall' and South West regionalisation have produced a Cornish institutional vacuum. Although MK began to alert people to this process consistently from the late 1960s onwards, its pleas went unheard or ignored. Policy-actors in Cornwall at first acquiesced, and then, after the 1970s, actively engaged in the piecemeal dismantling of Cornwall's institutional infrastructure. As this dismantling proceeded MK and other Cornish nationalists were not able to

convince enough people in Cornwall of the seriousness of its consequences. Now we are almost at the end point of this process. About
the only institution still based on the historic territory of Cornwall is
the County Council, itself left with precious little freedom following
central government 'reforms' of local government since the 1980s.
Tighter and tighter Whitehall control over Cornwall's local authorities has left them with little leeway to evolve the strategies or policies
that could build on distinctiveness. Even Cornwall's denuded County
Council is under threat as New Labour demands unitary 'local government' as the price for its 'regional government'. Decisions affecting Cornwall, both in the public as well as the private sector, are now
almost invariably made outside Cornwall.

But, even had there been more room for autonomous decision-making
in Cornwall's corridors of power, there is little evidence that this would
have led to policies designed to cope with Cornwall's particular and
unusual mix of socio-economic trends since the 1960s: chronic structural
economic problems caused by de-industrialisation plus high population
growth and associated growth pressures. For, as we have seen in this
book, the local political mainstream has repeatedly spurned a series of
opportunities to make a case for Cornish solutions. In doing this, it was
encouraged by a stream of policy studies that reinforced the accepted
taken-for-granted assumptions that all Cornwall needed to prosper were
wider roads, more people, greater investment, growth centres and all the
associated paraphernalia of 'development'. Furthermore, this had to happen within a framework of either Devon and Cornwall or 'South West'
planning. Cornwall was just too small to have any 'clout'.[2] In the absence
of a similar counter-weight of publications, the assumptions that lay
behind these studies were rarely questioned or subjected to rigorous
testing. Instead, 'opinion-formers' in Cornwall had had their opinions
formed by studies that usually downplayed Cornwall's potential economic and cultural strengths while ignoring its need for an institutional
structure of its own. Indeed, it is very possible that, without MK's campaigning, the process of administrative dismantling would have gone
even further and faster.

The problem may go deeper. Throughout the wider Cornish community there has been a lack of confidence in Cornwall and Cornish-derived
solutions, a mind-set that refuses to trust the ability of people in Cornwall to make decisions about their own communities, an attitude that
condemns Cornishness to the past and hurries, frantically and uncritically,
to align itself with the latest fashionable metropolitan remedy. This is a
cultural attitude shared by a section of both deeply 'Cornish' councillors
and newcomers. Both groups have been reluctant to look to Cornish
resources to solve Cornish problems; neither has dared to challenge the

preconceptions of the central state or the 'regionalisers' of the South West. As a result, opportunities to build the institutions that could give voice to a growing sense of Cornish identity have been thrown away. There are many examples; there was little widespread or convincing 'official' backing for a Cornish Euro-constituency in the late 1970s or for a Cornish-based TEC in the early 1990s; there was negligible support for Objective One funding until 1998 or a Cornish University until around the same time. The locally rooted civil society that could mobilise opinion on these issues just did not exist. In its absence MK and others have had to beat a lonely path in calling for such measures.

At the same time however, it could be argued that some of the actions of the wider Cornish 'Revival' and of MK in its early days helped to entrench this lack of self-confidence in Cornish governance – at least indirectly. Much of the national movement before the 1970s, and even later in some quarters, looked to the past for its inspiration. This was a perfectly understandable strategy in that there was a concern to 'collect the fragments' before the Cornish identity well and truly drowned in a global anonymity. But, for some, this orientation towards the past tended to become an obsession with the past. Many, perhaps even the majority, of the Revivalist movement in the 1950s and 1960s appeared to lose sight of Morton Nance's injunction that 'Old' Cornwall was a resource for a 'New' Cornwall. To some extent, this attitude gained strength from a more populist sense of nostalgia that became embedded in Cornish culture as rapid social changes began to wreak their effects after 1960. In the face of externally-triggered and seemingly uncontrollable change some Cornish people turned inwards, to the apparent certainties and assurances of their own families and places. But all this served to associate Cornishness over-much with the past, with a backward-looking and nostalgic world-view. A concern with Cornwall and with Cornish issues could, as a result, all too easily be portrayed as an obsession with things long gone, rather than as a perspective on the present and future. Some of the attitudes and positions adopted by the national movement in Cornwall, from the symbolic choice of the name 'Old Cornwall' in the 1920s to the cultural concerns of some Revivalists in the later 1950s and 1960s can be seen as reinforcing this image rather than dispelling it.

Associated with this has been a language that at times seems over-defensive. Backs to the wall rhetoric of Cornwall being threatened with extinction and of the 'end of Cornwall' has come easily to Cornish nationalists and re-appeared regularly, especially at times of crisis such as during the overspill debate of the 1960s, the in-migration of the 1970s and economic failures of the mid to late 1990s. To some extent this reflects the David and Goliath situation that Cornish nationalists find themselves in and the massive social changes that sometimes appear to be changing their land beyond recognition. Yet, while reflecting a more general malaise in Cornish society, on the other hand such defensiveness is sometimes over-dramatic and avoids the harder task of looking for opportunities rather than bemoaning threats. MK and Cornish nationalism in its first 50 years has been notably more effective when reacting against an external threat. Somehow, in the next 50 years, this has to become more pro-active, more confident and less defensive in order to engender a wider confidence and give the movement a wider base.

Yet, from another viewpoint, those same Revivalists who looked to the past for inspiration can be argued to have achieved the biggest success for the national movement in the long run. That small band of people in the 1950s and 1960s who published Cornish calendars, taught Cornish language classes and revived various local traditions in retrospect had a greater impact, albeit indirect, than their more politically-minded counterparts. As we have noted in this book, the inter-war Cornish Revival encountered difficulties in linking its vision of a Celtic, Cornish (speaking) Cornwall to a popular culture dominated by the leftovers of industrial society – mining, Methodism, rugby and Gladstonian Liberalism. In the 1970s this finally began to change.

Part of the reason may have been generational, as the older age groups, those most wedded to the traditional popular culture, passed on. But another reason was the activity of MK and cultural revivalists. They had constantly striven to keep the notion of a distinct 'Celtic' Cornish culture to the fore. By the 1980s and 90s this bore fruit, ironically precipitated by those massive cultural and social changes that had appeared to be such a threat in the 1970s. The feelings associated with emigration, of leaving one's land, have to some extent been generalised as Cornish people experience the eerie feeling of their land leaving them, as things change rapidly around them. Just as emigration could push people to re-assess their identity so contemporary social change pushed Cornish people to seek to differentiate themselves. The results included the widespread adoption of Celtic symbols and iconography as well as the more prosaic burrowing away in the family history archives as 'roots' were desperately sought. Perhaps most symbolic of this shift in popular culture in Cornwall has been the widespread promotion of St.Pirans's flag as the flag of Cornwall. As late as the 1970s this was vilified in some quarters as 'MK's flag' but just 20 years later even Cornwall County Council was proudly flying the flag, along with the European and Union flags, from their flagpoles at Truro.

Flag-waving and the popularity of other, less public 'Celtic' manifestations such as jewellery and Cornish music and dance are themselves measures of a more confident, more assertive identity and of a veritable Cornish cultural renaissance. Nevertheless, that identity has only fitfully spilt over into the political arena. One area in which Cornishness is more evident is single issue politics. At every protest in Cornwall the appearance of the Cornish flag now seems mandatory. To this extent the new social movements of protest in Cornwall are evidence of some seepage from the cultural to the political spheres.[3] Cornishness thus continues to be important in a defensive way, providing symbols of identity for local protest movements and bolstering resistance to attempts to compromise or destroy territorial integrity. But it has not fostered a clearly and consistently pro-active nationalist political activism. Cornishness is still seen as something cultural rather than political. We are visibly reminded of this at times of state ceremony such as the Queen Mother's death in 2002. The Cornish flag was quickly removed from official flagpoles – to be replaced by the Union Jack at half-mast. Those who decide about such matters presumably consider it inappropriate or bad taste to fly the Cornish flag at half-mast on such state occasions. Furthermore, to the chagrin of Cornish nationalists, a strong sense of Cornish identity for many people in Cornwall continues to co-exist with a county mentality, an acceptance that Cornwall, while Celtic, is also a part of England.

A multiplicity of approaches

In the introduction to this volume we noted the tension that most nationalist movements have – the dilemma of how to combine an appeal to the indigenous population with an openness to wider constituencies of support, to all those who happen to live in the national territory. In Cornish nationalism, this has been all the more acute because of the demographic changes that took place after the 1950s. This has resulted in probably only around half of the electorate being able to claim 'Cornish' family roots. For many, particularly the older generation of nationalist activists, there was an ever-present fear that the Cornishness of Cornwall would be eclipsed and its ideals lost. Indeed, in its early days MK was suspicious of non-Cornish members and its associate membership scheme was partly designed to ward off possible take-overs. By the 1970s, however, these defensive attitudes were being questioned. The debates of the early 1970s, when attempts to restrict membership only to those who could prove Cornish origins were defeated, can be seen as a turning point. In that decade MK began to adopt a more inclusive and 'civic' definition of Cornishness, recognising the contribution that recent incomers could make to the rejuvenation of Cornwall. Associate membership status was abolished and 'Cornish' was re-defined in ways that could include anyone living in Cornwall.

While MK, over the years, has become more inclusive, other parts of the Cornish national movement appear to cling to an ethnic nationalism. For example, superficially, the Stannary Parliament has also claimed a commitment to a 'multicultural' society. Yet, at the same time, it continues to project an image of holding to a more strident and ethnically based view of what it is to be Cornish.[4] In many respects the Stannary's concerns and activities have complemented those of a democratic political party like MK, as during the poll tax campaign and the direct action carried out in 2001 by the 'Stannary Three' against English Heritage. But there have also been numerous clashes. At the turn of the twenty-first century Stannary supporters argued vigorously that campaigning to request a 'regional' government from London compromised the existing legitimacy of Cornwall's Stannary rights and ignored the presence of its Parliament and courts. For MK activists, in an echo of the arguments of the mid-1970s, this was unrealistic and blithely ignored the actual state of public opinion in Cornwall. Moreover, it could be seen as merely another version of that familiar Cornish defeatism, carrying the implication that nationalists needed to do little in the public political sphere, just wait for Cornish rights to be recognised.

Differences between the emphasis to be given to ethnic and civic nationalism interweave with another long-running tension within the broader Cornish nationalist movement – whether to concentrate on electoral or pressure group politics. This feature of Cornish nationalism has sometimes led to an uncertain strategic response to events. MK began its life in the 1950s and 60s as a pressure group, open to members of other parties and contesting only the occasional election. As we have seen, it drifted into electioneering in the 1960s, encouraged by a small core of members who had always had the vision of building a national party and who were buoyed up by the wave of popular support over overspill. However, when that wave receded, doubts about this decision quickly re-surfaced. In the 1970s there remained within MK a large minority who had never whole-heartedly accepted an electoral strategy. In the 1980s, when people were, perhaps belatedly, discussing the long-term future of MK, the pressure group option was again raised. A range of pressure groups, sometimes operating inside MK, sometimes separate from it, have come and gone over the years. These have included groups such as Cowethas Flamank, Cornwall Against the Structure Plan (CASP), the Cornish Social and Economic Research Group (CoSERG) and the Cornish Bureau of European Relations (COBER). Even more recently, at the end of the 1990s, during which time MK itself had adopted a much more explicit electoral strategy, one response to the closure of South Crofty mine was the formation of the pressure group Cornish Solidarity. The aims of Cornish Solidarity were very close to the traditional demands of MK; the only difference was its emphasis on pressure group campaigning, a stance that brought it early success and considerable media coverage. However, this soon waned once the immediate 'crisis' had apparently disappeared.

The attraction of pressure group politics and of groups like Cornish Solidarity have been all the greater because of MK's failure to achieve an electoral breakthrough. MK has not yet achieved sufficient votes at parliamentary level to force itself to the attention of a wider audience. At this level its voting strength remains below the threshold of visibility and it is confined to that limbo of 'other parties'. Nonetheless, if we look at the record of local elections MK's vote has been much more respectable, producing the occasional councillor and fluctuating at a level far higher than that normally attained by 'fourth parties' in England such as the Greens, or for that matter the UDB in Brittany. Its level of voting support at local elections would, in other contexts and in other, more proportional, voting systems, be enough to guarantee a solid block of councillors and a far higher profile.

Indeed, its sustained local presence over more than 50 years can be viewed as an achievement in its own right. This longevity suggests a basic core of support for the idea of Cornish nationalism, albeit a limited one. But this has not, contrary to some fears in the 1950s and despite the major demographic and social shifts since the 1960s, withered away on a tide of suburbanisation and 'anglicisation'. The continued presence of the Cornish political movement and of MK has helped to put Cornish issues onto the agenda since the 1950s and to keep them there. In particular, it is unlikely that, without the existence of an active nationalist grouping, the Liberals and later Liberal Democrats in Cornwall would have appealed to such slogans as 'A Fair Deal for Cornwall' in their electioneering. While the rhetoric often exceeds the substance, the adoption of an 'anti-metropolitan' position by Liberalism in Cornwall has to some extent been the result of nationalist competition, as well as serving to trump the nationalists' potential ace. In fact the presence of Liberalism has been a constant background to MK's history, at certain crucial points limiting its growth. Possibly the most important period in this respect was the later 1960s. Unlike Scottish and Welsh nationalism MK was late into the electoral field. Because of the historical weakness of Labour in Cornwall the Liberals still occupied the position in most of Cornwall of main opposition party to the Tories and provided a more credible anti-metropolitan alternative to nationalism than it did in Scotland or Wales. Moreover, MK members were always in two minds whether to support the Liberals as the lesser of the London-orientated evils, or to oppose them as their biggest electoral threat. Attempts to distance MK from Liberalism more clearly in policy terms fell foul of the problem that the level of popular national consciousness in Cornwall was unable to sustain a very radical line. In consequence, MK has had to live with Liberal competition, one that restricts its electoral space similar to the way the Socialist Party in Brittany has restricted the space available to the UDB since the 1970s.

From culture to politics

A 'Celtic' and Cornish cultural renaissance has therefore accompanied a continuing migration of institutions out of Cornwall and an enfeebled civil society in Cornwall. Is it likely that this process will be reversed during MK's second half-century? Can the success in the cultural sphere be transferred into the political? And how might this happen?

The mind-set that views Cornwall as an 'English county' must remain the biggest problem facing MK if it is to achieve greater influence in Cornwall's political life. Until more people in Cornwall reject this representation, the demand for political devolution will remain an uphill struggle. Moreover, it means that mixed messages will continue to emanate from Cornwall. While MK and others campaign for a Cornish Assembly for example, based partly on Cornwall's historic identity and its sense of difference, others inevitably muddy this call by accepting Cornwall's status as a county or even by actively pressing on with support for a 'Devonwall' or South West agenda. This in turn allows central government to continue blithely ignoring Cornwall in its policies on regional government. Local complicity in the migration of institutions eastwards has weakened the ability to demand, clearly and consistently, the institutional re-building that MK and others argue Cornwall requires. These factors – local parochialism and defeatism on the part of the majority of the local political 'elite' plus a top-down regionalisation that ignores Cornwall – provide the biggest challenge to MK as it embarks on its second half-century.

All these factors help to prevent a wider acceptance of the policies and attitudes that have germinated within the nationalist movement. For, as well as providing a pole of Cornishness that serves to remind other parties of the existence of Cornwall, its history shows that MK has, more positively, continually prefigured demands and campaigns that have been later and belatedly adopted by other parties and organisations. It has, in short, often been well ahead of the field. For example, one of the very earliest demands of MK in the 1950s was for a Cornish University. After 40 years this was picked up by others and we now see the first, tentative and halting steps towards this vision in the Combined Universities in Cornwall initiative at Tremough. In its *What Cornishmen Can Do* pamphlet of 1968, MK put forward ideas for renewable energy, for quality and cultural tourism and for local food processing at least a decade or two before others in Cornwall were claiming to have 'discovered' these ideas. Individuals in MK and outside were noting that the policy of population growth had a negative effect on economic well-being in Cornwall well before this was slowly and reluctantly conceded by policy-makers after the late 1980s. MK was calling for political devolution to Cornwall decades before other politicians joined this campaign at the end of the 1990s. Similarly, in 2000, it was MK that launched the declaration campaign that resulted in 50,000 signatures backing the campaign for a Cornish Assembly. Earlier, MK had been among the first to call for Objective One status for Cornwall, realising in the early 1990s that economic indicators were inexorably drifting to the levels where Cornwall qualified for these handouts. But again, the constant highlighting by MK and Cornish nationalists of the insidious effects of 'Devonwall' and regionalisation have been vindicated as the fruits of gains such as Objective One cannot be fully enjoyed because of the migration of institutions (and managerial and clerical jobs) out of Cornwall.

The way in which these policies and attitudes were at first routinely condemned as extremist and unrealistic and then coolly adopted as the epitome of realism has been extremely frustrating for MK activists. Nevertheless, all is not doom and gloom. It is possible to perceive renewed opportunities for MK in the present political and social climate. For example, European politics appear to be marked by a process of party dispersion. Old stable voting patterns have become increasingly unpredictable. Voters appear more willing to experiment at certain times by voting for parties of the populist right, the far left, or for greens. Minority political parties have proliferated as a result. This volatility is to some extent held in check in Britain by its antiquated and disproportional first-past-the-post voting system. But, with PR voting systems being long used in Northern Ireland and now introduced for elections to the devolved Parliaments and Assemblies in Scotland, Wales, London as well as for European elections, the voting system is no longer so unquestionably revered. In such a context, windows of electoral opportunity are likely to appear and MK stand to benefit from this voter volatility. Achieving the threshold of electoral respectability no longer seems to be quite such a forlorn and hopeless task.

Secondly, the lobbying of the government over its implementation of the Charter for Regional and Minority Languages, the Framework Convention on the Protection of National Minorities and on behalf of a Cornish Assembly, has shown the possibilities of a multi-level campaigning strategy. MK can be seen as the electoral wing of a broad-based campaigning movement, one that adopts mass petitioning, letters to the press, direct lobbying of government departments and approaches to the EU to press its case. By probing at various institutional levels, from Brussels down to Truro, such campaigns can adopt a flexibility and continue to cause embarrassment to government agencies. Indeed this is one way of reading the Labour Government's response to the campaign for a Cornish Assembly. Its White Paper on regional government studiously avoided any mention of the word 'Cornwall'.[5] This was echoed a few days later when the Parliamentary Under-Secretary of State for Transport, Local Government and the Regions, Alan Whitehead, rather oddly also failed to mention the taboo word 'Cornwall' once, despite replying to a debate on regional government introduced by Andrew George, MP for St. Ives.[6] Once may be an oversight, but twice looks too much of a coincidence. Such reticence when faced by the 'Cornish problem' may indicate uncertainty as much as arrogant and disdainful dismissal. It might suggest that central government is unsure about how to respond to a multi-level and flexible campaigning style.

Finally, while we have argued in this book that the Cornish identity is strong in the cultural sphere it has yet to be seen in a more widespread way as a resource for governance. The resurgence of Cornish consciousness since the 1970s has to be the most hopeful sign for Cornish nationalism. Unlike the inter-war years and the middle decades of the twentieth century, when Cornishness was associated almost entirely with a retrospective nostalgia and a sense of loss, there are now signs that the Cornish identity can be mobilised in new and different ways. Culturally, the attachment of icons of Cornishness to elements of youth culture, in surfing or in music, opens up new and varied modes of 'being' Cornish. Economically, the lip service paid to Cornish culture in such things as Objective One strategies or cultural heritage strategies may still wait to be translated into visible results, but it is there nonetheless. Politically, the awareness of the possibilities of Cornwall's status as a European region opens up a new, more outward-looking dimension.

Only time will tell us whether these hints of a more inclusive, multi-faceted, open and outward-looking culture in Cornwall will blossom. Will they lead to a more confident demand for the right to make decisions about the future of Cornish communities in Cornwall? Will they help to build a future that uses rather than abuses the cultural and environmental resources that Cornwall offers? As the new century unfolds the answers to these questions will become a little clearer. But whatever happens, there is little doubt that Cornish nationalists will continue to play a key role in prodding and stimulating any process of transition, from a parochial, uncritical and inward-looking political culture to an open, democratic and culturally confident society.

Notes

1. Richard and Ann Jenkin (1965), *Cornwall: The Hidden Land*, Bracknell, p. 27.
2. See the publications of Plymouth Business School, notably the annual *The South West Economy: Trends and Prospects*, edited by Peter Gripaios (1991 onwards), or Michael Havinden, Jean Queniart and Jeffrey Stanyer (1991), *Centre and Periphery: Brittany and Cornwall & Devon Compared*, Exeter.
3. Our thanks to Malcolm Williams for reminding us of this important aspect.
4. See also John Angarrack (1999), *Breaking the Chains: Propaganda, Censorship, Deception and the Manipulation of Public Opinion in Cornwall*, Camborne.
5. Department of Transport, Local Government and the Regions (2002), *Your Region, Your Choice: Revitalising the English Regions*, London.
6. Hansard, 15 May 2002, Cols 265WH-286WH.

POSTSCRIPT

This book was completed at the end of 2002, in advance of district council elections which took place in May 2003 at the same time as the elections to the Welsh Assembly and Scottish Parliament.

May was not a particularly good month for Celtic nationalist parties in Britain. The SNP lost eight of its seats in the Scottish Parliament and Plaid Cymru failed to maintain the challenge it had mounted to Labour in 1999, even losing a leader in the process. Press coverage concentrated on these events, but in Cornwall things were different.

Mebyon Kernow successfully defended three district council seats and gained two new ones. Audrey Metcalfe (Illogan South) and Helene Ranson (Camborne South), increased MK's total number of councillors on principal authorities to six, with three in Kerrier alone. There were also two near-misses with Stuart Cullimore missing out by only 15 votes in Camborne West and Eileen Carter by less than 50 votes in Perranporth. Twelve MK members were also elected to town councils throughout Cornwall.

Though hardly a political earthquake, these elections marked a mini-breakthrough, with two elements that especially cheered party activists. First, the victory of Helene Ranson at Camborne South and the other strong votes in the Camborne area were the result of several years of solid, persistent, unheroic parish pump politics at local branch level. This slowly built up the profile of MK and convinced voters of its local commitment. In 1995 the sole MK candidate in Camborne could only win 17 per cent of the votes of the Labour victor. This time the MK vote in the same ward was 82 per cent that of the (Tory) poll-topper. The success for the Camborne branch was a contrast to the pattern of previous victories, almost always involving well known local candidates, whose poll success could sometimes look similar to that of Independent councillors. But the Camborne results marked a new pattern for MK, showing it could compete with the 'pavement politics' of the Liberal Democrats.

The second aspect that encouraged MK was the fact that in the eight seats across Cornwall where the party was opposed by Labour candidates it came out on top in five. Overall, after this round of elections, the Labour Party in Cornwall has just nine district councillors, only three more than MK. Despite being the party of government, Labour's weakness in Cornwall is indicated by the fact that they could only contest a quarter of Cornish council wards in 2003. At local government level at least it is no longer unrealistic for MK to consider the possibility it might become the third party of Cornwall.

Yet this dream needs tempering by a healthy dose of realism. MK is still a long way from providing a comprehensive coverage in terms of electoral intervention. The total number of MK candidates - at 25 - was only one more than at the previous round of district council elections in 1999 and the party could only manage to contest 17 per cent of the 115 wards. In this respect, it still resembles the SNP of the 1950s rather than the SNP of the 1970s. To be in a position to attain parity with the SNP or Plaid Cymru, MK requires a lot more branches across Cornwall active in the day to day politics of their communities. It also needs a clearer and more consistent strategy for elections, building on areas of relative strength and cultivating the patience required for the long haul. For this a more professional organisation will be essential. In particular, a greater income and a full-time organiser would do much to allow the party to mount a more serious challenge to the three 'London' parties in Cornwall.

Even then, success is not guaranteed to follow. Certain constraints still exist. It was noticeable that local press coverage of MK gains in the 2003 local elections was virtually non-existent. For example, the *Camborne Packet* could wrongly claim in the week after the election that all three 'main' parties made gains in Camborne while strangely forgetting to draw attention to the fact that MK had gained two seats in the area. In addition the two and three seat wards of the district council elections benefit MK. Strong local candidates can win the second or third votes of otherwise Labour or Liberal Democrat voters. It remains more difficult to achieve success in single seat elections.

Here, a comparison with the Scottish elections of 2003 is instructive. Both the Scottish Socialist Party and the Green Party were able to reap success and publicity from the proportional electoral system to the Scottish Parliament, winning six and seven seats respectively. And yet at local level, where first past the post continues, both parties are largely unrepresented. The Green Party does not have one councillor on a unitary authority in Scotland while the Socialists fought 340 wards in the May elections, but won only two. In the absence of proportional representation the voting system in Cornwall likewise works against MK.

On a broader level the future of MK and Cornish nationalism more generally is still bound up with other developments. Much depends on whether the momentum achieved around the Cornish Constitutional Convention is continued into the 21st century. The Cornish movement has to convince people in Cornwall of the need for institutions that are based on Cornwall. If that happens confidence in Cornish solutions to Cornish problems should begin to increase and demands for political change become more insistent. That may, in turn, generate a more vital 'civil society' in Cornwall, one where strategies and policies can be critically and openly discussed, properly debated and locally owned. Only then will the cultural regeneration that has begun to open up in the past two decades be linked to civic renewal.

The future of MK and of Cornish nationalism more widely remains difficult to predict. Will MK be able to build on its progress in 2003 and establish itself as a serious electoral competitor? Will it consolidate its position as the public face of Cornish nationalism or will it be merely one of a number of competing voices? And will it achieve that potential noted by some political commentators: that 'it is a serious and committed presence on the Cornish scene with potential for growth'? Only time will tell.

Appendix

SOME LEADING PERSONALITIES IN CORNISH NATIONALISM

Helena Charles (1911–1997)

Helena Sanders (nee Charles) was Mebyon Kernow's first Chair and also the first MK member to win a seat on a local authority. Born in Calcutta of Cornish parents, she was a graduate of Oxford University. A passionate Christian socialist, she was in the fortunate position of being of independent means and spent most of her life in voluntary work. In the 1920s she worked in the slums of Bermondsey and during the Second World War she joined the London Ambulance Service. Helena was also well known for her selfless work on behalf of Jewish refugees during the war and in the immediate post-war period. When visiting Venice in 1964, she was so saddened by the large number of emaciated stray cats in the city that she co-founded a charity concerned with cat welfare. It was called Dingo – named after a friend's dog. For this work in Venice, she was made a Knight of St. Mark by the city. She also founded the Cornwall Christian Fellowship for Animals and the Cornwall Cat Rescue Group.

Major Cecil Beer (1902–1998)

MK's second Chairman Major Beer was a civil servant who had worked for the War Office and the Post Office Savings Bank prior to the Second World War, when he served in the Royal Artillery. He later become Provost Marshall over a large part of India as that country moved towards independence and returned to Britain in 1946, when he worked as the Meals Organisation Officer for South Wales. His links with the Cornish movement went back to the 1930s, when he was secretary of Tyr ha Tavas and organised the first service in revived Cornish at Towednack Church. Made a bard in 1934, Map Kenwyn rose to the position of Deputy Grand Bard from 1967 to 1972, serving under two Grand Bards, George

Pawley White and Denis Trevanion. Major Beer worked for Cornwall throughout his life, even during the ten years when he lived in Australia. While there, he was involved in the promotion of an Assembly of Australian Cornish Bards.

Ernest George Retallack Hooper (1908–1998)

E.G.R. Hooper was elected Honorary President of Mebyon Kernow in 1973, but is remembered primarily as a leading pioneer of the Cornish language revival. Known to most people simply by his bardic name Talek (meaning broad browed), he was made a bard of the Cornish Gorseth in 1932 and became the third Grand Bard, serving from 1959 to 1964. He had learnt Cornish from another pioneering stalwart A.S.D. Smith (Caradar) and communicated with colleagues in the language movement during the Second World War when he was based in Gibraltar. Following the war, he was encouraged by his wife Bertha to join her in the teaching profession. After training at Trinity College, Carmarthen, Talek and Bertha endeavoured to teach their pupils as much about Cornish history and language as they could. He also edited the magazine *An Lef Kernewek* (The Cornish Voice) for a total of 17 years, giving aspiring writers the opportunity to publish their works in Cornish. A founder member of MK, Talek had previously been one of the more political members of Tyr ha Tavas and participated in MK's early election campaigns in the 1960s, when Bertha twice contested elections to the Camborne-Redruth UDC.

Robert Dunstone (1922–1973)

Robert Dunstone was elected Chairman of Mebyon Kernow in 1960, leading the organisation through a period when it stood its first official election candidates, before becoming MK's first Honorary President in 1968. A civil servant, experienced in trade union matters, he was able to introduce a new strand into the movement's support. Like many Falmouth boys, he worked in the town's docks, first as an office boy and then latterly as a ships joiner. It was here that he became interested in trade union matters, and he continued as an activist throughout his life, later serving as secretary of Truro's Trade Council. In the 1940s, he served as a regular soldier in the Duke of Cornwall's Light Infantry, the Devonshire Regiment and the Royal Army Signal Corps, ending up as a staff sergeant and chief clerk. Returning to Cornwall he lived in Truro, naming his house 'Smithick' – a traditional name for Falmouth. A very religious man, he also served his church as a Sunday School teacher, parish worker and then also as a Diocesan reader.

Len Truran (1926–1996)

A local headteacher, Len Truran served MK as both National Secretary and Chairman during the organisation's period of greatest growth in the 1960s and 1970s, also standing in the 1979 General Election for Falmouth-Camborne. Leonard's brother Lambert had been a founder member of Mebyon Kernow, while Len did not join the new movement until he was convinced that it had the potential to serve Cornwall. Elected Chairman in 1968 he returned in 1973 to the post of National Secretary where he felt in closer touch with members and branches. Throughout the 1970s he promoted a well-organised sales operation with items such as stamps and calendars being used to produce funds and also publicise Mebyon Kernow and its objectives. Len left MK in 1980, following the disputes within the party at that time, and then built up the book firm Dyllansow Truran, which became well-known for Cornish histories, poetry, language courses as well as reprints of Cornish classics. It has been estimated that he published well over 200 books. In the early 1980s, he became a leading light in the Social Democratic Party in the Falmouth and Camborne constituency, but rejoined MK in 1990.

Richard Jenkin (1925–2002)

The highlight of MK's 1998 Party Conference was the generous and heartfelt tribute paid to MK stalwart Richard Jenkin, who was awarded the honorary title of Life President at the event. Born in Manchester in 1925, Richard Garfield Jenkin was the son of a Mousehole man who had to leave Cornwall to find work, eventually becoming a clergyman. In 1947 Richard became a language bard of the Cornish Gorseth in 1947 and took the bardic name 'Map Dyvroeth' – son of exile. Richard studied Chemistry at Manchester University and then taught at Plymouth, Monmouthshire and Totnes before settling in Leedstown in 1960 to teach at Helston School. A founder member of Mebyon Kernow, he served as Party Chairman between 1973 and 1983 and achieved many firsts for the party. He was MK's first parliamentary candidate in 1970 and also the first member to contest an election to the European Parliament, when he polled nearly 10 per cent of the Cornish vote. As well as being active in Mebyon Kernow, he held positions of responsibility in a wide range of Cornish organisations including the Celtic Congress, the Cornish Language Board and the Federation of Old Cornwall Societies. Richard also served as Grand Bard on two separate occasions between 1976–1982 and 1985–1988.

Colin Murley

Colin Murley won MK's first-ever county council seat at St. Day and Lanner in April 1967. Living in Hayle at the time and working for West Penwith Rural District Council, Colin took the field against a well-known pro-overspill candidate and defeated him by three votes. In his election address, he wrote 'we do not want amalgamation, take-over bids or the dictation of final solutions from Whitehall. An obsession with centralisation has deprived our Cornish Nation of much vitality and self-respect'. Colin joined the fledgling Cornish National Party as its treasurer in 1969 but subsequently rejoined MK and polled the party's best-ever General Election result in the St. Ives constituency in 1979. He contested a number of local elections in the Penzance/St. Just area between 1970 and 1985 but was forced to spend much of the 1980s working outside Cornwall, including spells in Papua New Guinea and Saudi Arabia. Since coming back to Cornwall, Colin has become one of the leading activists in the Cornish Stannary Parliament.

Roger Holmes

The geologist son of a Liskeard GP, Roger has served his home town of Liskeard as an elected councillor for over thirty years. He is also the only person to have fought elections as an official MK candidate in each of the last five decades. He was first elected onto Liskeard Borough Council in 1968 at the age of 23. Following the local government reorganisation of 1973, Roger was then returned to both Caradon District Council and Liskeard Town Council. He served on the district council until 1983 and has remained on the town council until the present day. He also had the honour of being the town's mayor in millennium year. Roger was leader of the first Cornish National Party which broke away from MK in 1969, but he rejoined MK in the mid-70s and fought the Bodmin (South-East Cornwall) seat at the 1979 General Election. Roger is a passionate advocate of increased European co-operation and, in recent years, has been the driving force behind CoBER (Cornish Bureau for European Relations), through which he has sought to build links between Cornwall and other European nations and regions.

James Whetter

Born into an old Cornish family at Gorran, Dr James Whetter is a respected local historian who has produced works on Cornwall in the 13th
to 17th centuries, the Bodrugan family, Gorran Haven and Glasney College at Penryn. In Mebyon Kernow, Dr Whetter rose to the rank of Party
Vice-Chairman in the early 1970s, twice fighting the parliamentary seat of
Truro in 1974 and editing the party magazine *Cornish Nation* from 1970
to 1975. He left MK in 1975 and formed the Cornish Nationalist Party,
following a failed attempt to be elected Party Chairman. Dr Whetter has
served as the Chairman of the CNP since its inception and fought a
number of elections for the party between 1979 and 1985 including the
parliamentary seats of Truro and North Cornwall and a number of council
wards. He is presently working on plans for an archaeological excavation
on the site of Penryn's Glasney College, which was the centre of Cornish
learning in the Middle Ages, as well as various other historical projects.

Julyan Drew

Julyan was the most prominent member of the Drew family from Penzance,
who were all very active MK members in the late 1970s and early 1980s.
Elected to serve as Chairman between 1983 and 1985, Julyan Drew was a
very effective election organiser. He acted as agent for Colin Murley in
his 1979 parliamentary campaign and many candidates standing in local
elections, including long-standing councillor Colin Lawry. He stood as a
candidate himself on a number of occasions and throughout his period
of leadership, the high-profile team of election activists in West Cornwall
were nicknamed the 'Drew's Militia'. From the left of the party, Julyan
was also a leading light in the 1913 Group founded in 1981. A social
worker during his time in MK, he is now a Methodist Minister serving the
communities of Newlyn and Mousehole.

Pedyr Prior

Pedyr Prior was elected Party Chairman in 1985, a position he held for one
year. Pedyr first came to prominence in the Cornish movement in February 1976 as a member of the recently-formed Cornish Nationalist Party,
when he was selected as its parliamentary candidate for St. Ives. He made
headlines one month later, publicly standing down in favour of the MK
candidate for the constituency. Soon after this, Pedyr joined MK and

became one of its most committed election campaigners, fighting the St. Ives constituency himself in 1983. In total, he contested ten council elections in St. Ives and Porthleven between 1977 and 1989, serving on Porthleven Town Council for a number of years. Pedyr also served the party for two spells as National Secretary and co-edited *Cornish Nation* magazine in the late 1970s, as well as *Carn*, the journal of the Celtic League. He was also prominent in the anti-poll tax movement of 1990 and helped organise the first protest march against the tax outside Scotland.

Loveday Carlyon

The reins of the party leadership were in the hands of Loveday Carlyon between 1986–1989. Originally active in MK's Torpoint branch, she moved to Liskeard and married stalwart MK member Julyan Holmes, brother of MK councillor Roger Holmes. Soon after she was elected onto the local town council. She was a founding member of CASP and also promoted a series of other high profile media campaigns – including the need to support local food producers. She had a particular success on the issue of Cornish language road signs. In 1988, the Department of Transport ruled that the Cornish language wording on road signs outside Liskeard had to be removed in order to reduce potential confusion for motorists. Loveday built a local coalition, including the local Chamber of Commerce, to fight the move. This forced the government to back down and acknowledge the legitimate use of the language on local signage, at the same time making it possible for many other Cornish towns to use the language.

Colin Lawry

Newlyn's Colin Lawry holds the mantle as Mebyon Kernow's most successful campaigner at the ballot box. He first stood for the party in the Cornwall County Council elections of 1981 at the age of only twenty-one. On this occasion he lost out by only 81 votes, pushing the sitting councillor into third place. One year later Colin was elected onto Penwith District Council (Penzance Central) and in 1985 also won election onto Cornwall County Council (Penzance South), serving on that authority until 2001. Colin Lawry has had many roles within MK, ranging from assistant treasurer in the early 1980s through to Vice-Chairman (west) and Deputy Leader in more recent years. Throughout the 1980s and 1990s, Colin played a leading role in the campaign for a Cornwall-only

European parliamentary constituency. In 2000, he chaired a working group which commissioned a report calling for the recognition of the Cornish people as a 'national minority'. Colin Lawry works in Truro's Magistrates Court, and also represented his fellow workers as their union representative for many years.

Loveday Jenkin

Loveday, the daughter of Richard and Ann Jenkin, was elected Party Chairman in 1990 and her seven years of leadership were important in rebuilding MK as a political party, willing to enter electoral politics at all levels. Loveday herself fought the 1994 elections to the European Parliament and soon after was returned as councillor for her home parish of Crowan on Kerrier District Council. Trained as a plant biochemist at the Universities of Cardiff and Cambridge, she worked for a number of years with a Cornish nature conservation charity. She presently lectures in environmental waste management at the world-renowned Camborne School of Mines. A bard of the Cornish Gorseth, Loveday is also a dedicated campaigner for the Cornish language. She runs local classes in the Camborne area and has served on both the Cornish Language Board and the Cornish Language Fellowship. Both her children have Cornish as a first language.

Dick Cole

Dick Cole was MK's Press and Campaigns Officer from 1992 to 1997, when he succeeded Loveday Jenkin as Party Chairman. Formerly a farmworker, he left Cornwall in 1988 to study at St. Davids University College in Lampeter, where he gained valuable political experience with Plaid Cymru in Ceredigion. Since his return to Cornwall, Dick helped to orchestrate a considerable increase in the electoral impact of Mebyon Kernow, bringing the number of local election candidates to an all-time high and in 1999, he was elected to represent his home parish of St. Enoder on Restormel Borough Council. Dick was also one of the three founders of the cross-party Cornish Constitutional Convention in July 2000 and served the body as its Vice-Chairman for its first two years. Dick also wrote and produced the 'Declaration for a Cornish Assembly', which has been signed by over 50,000 people. He is an archaeologist and works for the Cornwall Archaeological Unit.

Allin-Collins, R St V 27

INDEX

SUPPORTING SUBSCRIBERS

Aitken Ab Ieuan, Strathclyde, Scotland.
Patti Akrigg, Pensilva, Kernow/Cornwall.
Jane Acton, Porthleven, Kernow/Cornwall.
Cllr. Barry Andrew, Truro, Kernow/Cornwall.
Fr. Paul Andrew, London, England.
John Osborne Angwin, Braunton, England.
Pauline Barnes, Godolphin Cross, Kernow/Cornwall.
John H Bath, Plymouth, England.
Janet Bentley, Walsall, England.
Cllr. Bert Biscoe, Truro, Kernow/Cornwall.
Cllr. John Bolitho, Bude, Kernow/Cornwall.
Duncan Champion, Seaton, Kernow/Cornwall.
Michael and Margaret Cole, St Dennis Junction, Kernow/Cornwall.
Cllr. Stuart Cullimore and Cllr. Helene Ranson, Troon, Kernow/Cornwall.
Devolve!, Leicester, England.
Rev. Julyan Drew. Penzance, Kernow/Cornwall.
Chris Dunkerley, New South Wales, Australia.
David Ford, Padstow, Kernow/Cornwall.
The late Ron Greet, Killarney, Ireland.
Dr. Amy Hale, Lanbrebois, Kernow/Cornwall.
Cllr. Philip Hills, Camborne, Kernow/Cornwall.
Cllr. Paul Holmes, Illogan, Kernow/Cornwall.
Cllr. Roger Holmes, Liskeard, Kernow/Cornwall.
Ann Trevenen Jenkin, Leedstown, Kernow/Cornwall.
Conan Jenkin, Truro, Kernow/Cornwall.
Cllr. Dr. Loveday Jenkin, Praze-an-Beeble, Kernow/Cornwall.
The late Richard Jenkin, Leedstown, Kernow/Cornwall.
Dr. Alan M Kent, Lanbrebois, Kernow/Cornwall.
Colin and Denise Lawry, Newlyn, Kernow/Cornwall.
Catherine Lorigan, Reading, England.
Raymond Lyford, Llanelli, Wales.
John Manley, St. Germans, Kernow/Cornwall.
Carole Mann, Perranporth, Kernow/Cornwall.
William McCallum, Glasgow, Scotland.
Les McInulty, Isle of Lewis, Scotland.
Les Merton, Redruth, Kernow/Cornwall.
Sister Elizabeth Morris, Kettering, England.

Nigel Nethersole, Redruth, Kernow/Cornwall.
Cllr. Ronald Overd, West Looe, Kernow/Cornwall.
Johnathan Pallett, Taunton, England.
Barbara Panvel, Solihull, England.
Keith Pascoe, Camborne, Kernow/Cornwall.
Kenneth Lanyon Pascoe, Twelveheads, Kernow/Cornwall.
John Pearce, West Calder, Scotland.
Andrew Penhaligan, Millbrook, Kernow/Cornwall.
Dr. R J Pentreath, Bath, England.
Ingrid Pratt (nee Prior), Padstow, Kernow/Cornwall.
Frank Rankin, Glasgow, Scotland.
Cllr. Phil Rendle, Gulval, Kernow/Cornwall.
Gary Retallick, London, England.
Andrew Roberts, West Sussex, England.
Colin Roberts, Stoke on Trent, England.
David Robins, Weston-super-Mare, England.
J P R Rogers, Sandhurst, England
Ian Saltern, Stratton, Kernow/Cornwall.
Graham Sandercock, Liskeard, Kernow/Cornwall.
Cllr. Alan, Gillian and Martin Sanders, Troon, Kernow/Cornwall.
Roy and Patricia Schama, Philleigh, Kernow/Cornwall.
Patrick Semmens, St Just, Kernow/Cornwall.
Kenneth Sibley, Skegness, England.
Adrian Spalding, Praze-an-Beeble, Kernow/Cornwall.
Prof. Matthew Spriggs, Canberra, Australia.
B G Staddon, Swindon, England.
Graham Symmons, Stithians, Kernow/Cornwall.
Rhisiart Tal-e-bot, Truro, Kernow/Cornwall.
R H Tennent, Porthleven, Kernow/Cornwall.
Rita Thompson, London, England.
Kevin Trebell, Lanner, Kernow/Cornwall.
Tom Tremewan, Perranporth, Kernow/Cornwall.
Julie Trevithick, Kingskerswell, England.
Elizabeth-Carole Twist, Blackwater, Kernow/Cornwall.
Cllr. Hilda Wasley, Threemilestone, Kernow/Cornwall.
George Pawley White, Camborne, Kernow/Cornwall.
Derek Williams, Oswestry, England.
Justin and Marie Williams, Redruth, Kernow/Cornwall.
Malcolm Williams, Saltash, Kernow/Cornwall.
Warner Williams, Birkenhead, England.